Married Ever After

ALI HAMMUDA

Married Ever After

First published in England by
Kube Publishing Ltd,
Markfield Conference Centre,
Ratby Lane, Markfield,
Leicestershire LE67 9SY,
United Kingdom.

Distributed by
Kube Publishing Ltd.
Tel: +44(0)1530 249230
Email: info@kubepublishing.com
www.kubepublishing.com

ISBN 978-1-84774-239-1 Paperback
ISBN 978-1-84774-240-7 ebook

Editor: Zimarina Sarwar
Cover design and typesetting: Afreen Fazil (Jaryah Studios)
Printed by: Elma Basim, Turkey

Contents

As you navigate challenges

As you dissolve the marriage

Introduction

When you hear the word "marriage", what comes to mind?

For many people, their thoughts turn to the kind of marriage they would like to have or the type they have witnessed growing up. Others may think of the state of the marriage they are currently in, or perhaps one they have left behind.

Since the dawn of mankind, marriage has existed – across cultures and geographic boundaries – as the public union of a man and woman who are thereafter to be recognised as a couple. Whether you marry and who you choose to marry are arguably one of the most impactful decisions of your adult life. This relationship will see you through all the varied seasons of life – from those initial exciting moments of sharing all of yourself with another person to experiencing parenthood together, making decisions about work, travel, careers, or even suffering illness or the death of family and friends. The quality of your marital bond can be the vessel in which you weather the storms of life, allowing you to have constant support by your side against the elements beyond your control.

However, like all human endeavours, the success of a marriage hinges on a variety of factors, including the attitude, willingness, and commitment of the people involved, the support networks at hand, and the framework a couple turn to when in need of guidance and direction. As with many matters in life, the results one attains is often a reflection of the effort put in. Our lives are a journey with many unexpected twists and turns, and marriage is no exception to this. However, as with all journeys, we must equip ourselves with the necessary provisions for the path. You will draw upon these provisions not only when the road is rocky or takes an unexpected detour, but also when it is smooth and the view ahead appears beautiful.

Essentially, your life is simply a cosmic journey, and marriage is the key to facilitate the ease of undertaking this journey until you both reach your ultimate destination – the Pleasure of Allah ﷻ.

In this book, you will find twenty Qur'anic principles to guide you through the different stages of the marital process. Each of these principles will be contextualised with Prophetic examples and contemporary research on the study of successful marriages. Topics will include preparing for marriage with the right attitude, maintaining harmony once married, navigating the inevitable challenges that come with marriage, and – when necessary – the etiquette of ending a marriage in the best of ways.

These principles are aspirational goals we should strive to understand, implement, and maintain – *especially* when the lowest parts of ourselves do not want to. As humans we will often fall short, however, we will find success when we rise, redirect, and refocus on the principles sent to us in a Book without flaw.

The irony of life is that every path you choose will contain its own challenges. You may find that, as "difficult" as it is to live by the principles of this book, it is actually much harder not to. There will be struggles in both directions, but it is up to you to pick the struggle that is worthy, rewarding and leads to the highest level of contentment.

Use this book as a guide, a frequent reminder, and a compass leading you back to Divine Pleasure. The sincere intention of working, striving, and struggling to live by the principles contained here will bring success not only to your marriage, but to your very soul.

Some disclaimers

1. Manage your expectations

It is important to manage your expectations in a realistic way from the outset. As such, you should remember that minor day-to-day issues were never entirely eradicated even from the household of the Prophet ﷺ. This is simply the reality of life. This book seeks to address the overall principles that bring harmony to marriage and to guard against the most serious issues threatening to destroy the marital bond. Our lives will not be perfect, and human conduct will always be marred by shortcomings. So, for the smaller niggles of life, we must overlook such trifling annoyances and be patient in order to preserve the bigger picture.

2. Patience is never lost

The Chinese bamboo tree provides us with a remarkable lesson from nature. After its seed is sown, a minuscule shoot is all that is visible for four years. What is unseen during all these years is the vast and intricate root network developing beneath the soil. Then, in its fifth year, the Chinese bamboo tree emerges in full force, skyrocketing up to 80 feet in height.

Life and relationships often mirror the growth pattern of this unique tree. There might be times when, despite your continuous efforts and dedication, you may see little to no external progress. Doubt may lay its roots, testing your resolve. But as is the case with the bamboo tree, perseverance and faith can lead to an explosive period of growth and realisation. It is essential to remember that even when results are not immediate or evident, your dedication is not in vain. Brighter days often lie ahead, waiting for better moments to reveal themselves.

3. View marriage as one part of a wide support network

Marriage is undoubtedly one of the most important relationships in your life, but no human relationship should be relied on to fulfil your every single need. Whilst your spouse will *in shā' Allāh* bring you much relief and solace, it is crucial to recognise that relying solely on one person to fulfil all of your needs can lead to unmet expectations, disappointment, and potential strain on the relationship itself. It is important to have a network of relationships, including family, friends and community, each providing different types of support and fulfilling different needs.

To elaborate, friendships can provide emotional support, a sense of belonging, and companionship outside of the marital relationship. Family relationships can provide a sense of heritage, tradition, and connection to one's roots. Community relationships can provide a sense of purpose, shared values, and a sense of contributing to something larger than oneself.

People have diverse needs and desires that extend beyond the scope of any single individual. We have emotional, social, intellectual, and spiritual dimensions that require nurturing and fulfilment. By cultivating relationships with family, friends, and the wider community, we open ourselves up to a variety of experiences, perspectives, and sources of joy.

Moreover, nurturing other relationships alongside marriage helps create a well-rounded support system. During challenging times, it can be beneficial to have multiple sources of solace, guidance, and advice. Each relationship brings its own strengths, and by fostering connections beyond your spouse, you can ensure that your emotional well-being is not solely dependent on one person.

A DIVINE LINK

Marriage and Your Life's Purpose

Have you ever wondered what exists within marriage, and its greatness, that we tie it to the very purpose of our lives? There are several key similarities between these two things:

Tawḥīd (the Unity of Allah ﷻ)

As Muslims, we are aware of what *tawḥīd* generally means: the Unity of Allah ﷻ as One, Indivisible, and the Independent Lord. It is at the very core of our lives, as evidenced by how the Prophet ﷺ instructed Muʿādh ibn Jabal رضي الله عنه when he was sent to Yemen:

فَلْيَكُنْ أَوَّلُ مَا تَدْعُوهُمْ إِلَيْهِ شَهَادَةَ أَنْ لَا إِلَهَ إِلَّا اللهُ وَأَنَّ مُحَمَّدًا رَسُولُ اللهِ

Start by inviting them to testify that there is no god but Allah, and that Muhammad is the Messenger of Allah.[1]

Marriage is one institution that demonstrates the distinction between the Independent, Supreme and Sovereign nature of Allah ﷻ and the dependent state of humans who crave, desire and struggle without constant intimate companionship.

[1] Al-Bukhārī, *Ṣaḥīḥ al-Bukhārī.*

Allah ﷻ says about Himself:

وَأَنَّهُ تَعَالَى جَدُّ رَبِّنَا مَا اتَّخَذَ صَاحِبَةً وَلَا وَلَدًا

And He, exalted is the majesty of our Lord, has not taken for himself a wife nor a son.[2]

In absolute contrast to Him, human beings struggle without the relief and comfort of a spouse from our own kind, due to our deep and natural yearning for love, companionship, and support.

This is why Allah ﷻ says:

هُوَ الَّذِي خَلَقَكُم مِّن نَّفْسٍ وَاحِدَةٍ وَجَعَلَ مِنْهَا زَوْجَهَا لِيَسْكُنَ إِلَيْهَا

It is He who created you from one soul and then from it He created its partner so that he may find rest in her.[3]

From this simple reflection alone, we can appreciate why marriage itself is a sign of "*Qul huwa Allāhu aḥad*" (*Say, "He is Allah, The Only One"*).[4] This is an indication of the Oneness of Allah ﷻ, the Independence of Allah ﷻ, the Self-reliance of Allah ﷻ, the Wholeness of Allah ﷻ, and the Incomparable Nature of Allah ﷻ in regard to any of His creation. So, in marriage, we find clear reminders of *tawḥīd.*

Ittibāʿ: Conformity to the Way of the Prophet of Allah ﷺ

Following the Sunnah is indispensable in the journey to Allah ﷻ and the home of the Hereafter; since every other door to Allah ﷻ is shut without it. Again, this too is apparent within the institution of marriage.

---

[2] *Al-Jinn*, 72:3.
[3] *Al-Aʿrāf*, 7:189.
[4] *Al-Ikhlāṣ*, 112:1.

Anas ibn Mālik رضي الله عنه narrated:

A group of three men came to the houses of the wives of the Prophet ﷺ asking how the Prophet ﷺ worshipped, and when they were informed about that, they considered their worship insufficient and said, "Where are we in relation to the Prophet ﷺ, who has had his past and future sins forgiven!"

Then one of them said, "I will offer the prayer throughout the night forever." The other said, "I will fast throughout the year and will not break my fast." The third said, "I will keep away from women and will not ever marry."

Allah's Messenger ﷺ came to them and said:

أَنْتُمُ الَّذِينَ قُلْتُمْ كَذَا وَكَذَا؟ أَمَا واللهِ إِنِّي لأَخْشَاكُمْ للهِ وَأَتْقَاكُمْ لَهُ لَكِنِّي
أَصُومُ وَأُفْطِرُ وأُصَلِّي وَأَرْقُدُ وَأَتَزَوَّجُ النِّسَاءَ فَمَنْ رَغِبَ عَنْ سُنَّتِي فَلَيْسَ مِنِّي

Are you the same people who said So-and-so? By Allah, I am the most fearful of Allah and conscious of Him, yet I fast and break my fast, I pray and I sleep, and I also marry women. So he who does not follow my tradition in religion, is not from me.[5]

Marriage is seen as a natural, integral, and positive aspect of a Muslim's spiritual state that actions like celibacy and monasticism are viewed as an aberration and an "extreme" behaviour. Despite the zeal of these three men to free themselves of "worldly" pleasures so they could increase their worship, the Messenger of Allah ﷺ rebalanced their perspective by citing his own life and practice as the supreme example. It is the Mercy of Allah ﷻ that allows us to experience both the physical and emotional comfort marriage brings, and to deny this to yourself is akin to rejecting the Prophetic path.

[5] Al-Bukhārī, *Ṣaḥīḥ al-Bukhārī*.

Tazkiyah: Purification of the Soul

Tazkiyah is the regular, life-long practice of purifying your soul from everything that prevents you from reaching Allah's Pleasure. This involves aspects of internal work such as regular reflection, self-accountability, repentance and managing sinful desires.

Allah ﷻ said:

جَنَّاتُ عَدْنٍ تَجْرِي مِنْ تَحْتِهَا الْأَنْهَارُ خَالِدِينَ فِيهَا
وَذَٰلِكَ جَزَاءُ مَنْ تَزَكَّىٰ

The Gardens of Eternity, under which rivers flow, where they will stay forever. That is the reward of those who purify themselves.[6]

Yet again, marriage is a space which gives ample room for the manifestation of *tazkiyah* in an effective and meaningful way. Participating in a life partnership with your spouse carries an immediate practical benefit of providing you with a wholesome outlet for physical desire. In a world of hyper-sexualisation, the simple act of enjoying intimacy with your spouse will protect you from countless external harms that exist in wider society.

The Prophet ﷺ said:

يَا مَعْشَرَ الشَّبَابِ مَنْ اسْتَطَاعَ الْبَاءَةَ فَلْيَتَزَوَّجْ
فَإِنَّهُ أَغَضُّ لِلْبَصَرِ وَأَحْصَنُ لِلْفَرْجِ

O young men, whoever of you is able to marry, then let him get married; for it will help him lower his gaze and guard his chastity.[7]

Alongside this practical benefit, marriage fills a void in your heart, as the contentment within your home will allow you to focus on other important areas of life. If two people know that home is a sanctuary and place of rest, then they will feel

[6] *Ṭāhā*, 20:76.
[7] Al-Bukhārī, *Ṣaḥīḥ al-Bukhārī*.

equipped to tackle the challenges of life outside of it. Marriage allows you to assess the state of your heart and actions responding to your spouse's feelings. As a married person, you are bound to a lifelong commitment with someone whose thoughts, feelings, dreams, and aspirations are to be respected and shared with you. The heart of another human being is now vulnerable to your attentive consideration. How you respond to your spouse's needs will teach you lessons about yourself that you could not have gained elsewhere. The growth of your relationship will reveal to you the very best and worst of your character. As the person who gets to know you better than anyone else – and who spends the most time with you – your spouse will be able to give you the most accurate reflection of your character. When done with kindness and received likewise, this is one of the greatest tools you have to your self-development and spiritual purification.

The three key aspects of belief that every Muslim lives by – the Oneness of Allah, conformity to the Sunnah, and the purification of the soul – are all effortlessly contained within marriage. They manifest themselves in the most beautiful way within marriage, and therefore, this relationship is your life's greatest potential source of spiritual gain.

It is for this reason that the Prophet ﷺ said:

إِذَا تَزَوَّجَ العَبْدُ (وَفِي لَفْظٍ: مَنْ رَزَقَهُ اللهُ امْرَأَةً صَالِحَةً) فَقَدْ اِسْتَكْمَلَ نِصْفَ الدِّينِ فَلْيَتَّقِ اللهَ فِي النِّصْفِ البَاقِي

If a person gets married (another narration adds "whoever is blessed with a righteous woman"), he would have completed half of his religion, and so let him fear Allah with regard to the remaining half.[8]

[8] Al-Bayhaqī, *Al-Sunan al-Kubrā li al-Bayhaqī.*

AT A GLANCE

What is marriage?

1. The way of the Prophets before us

Allah ﷻ said:

وَلَقَدْ أَرْسَلْنَا رُسُلًا مِنْ قَبْلِكَ وَجَعَلْنَا لَهُمْ أَزْوَاجًا وَذُرِّيَّةً

And indeed We sent Messengers before you (O Muhammad) and made for them wives and offspring.[9]

This revelation serves to highlight the human nature of the Prophets, demonstrating that their lives encompassed the same human experiences and relationships as their followers, which should be recognised and emulated.

2. An indispensable garment

In a concise yet profound analogy, the Qur'an describes spouses:

هُنَّ لِبَاسٌ لَّكُمْ وَأَنتُمْ لِبَاسٌ لَّهُنَّ

They are garments for you and you are garments for them.[10]

[9] *Al-Ra'd*, 13:38.
[10] *Al-Baqarah*, 2:187.

Qatādah ﷺ said in explanation of this verse:

هُنَّ سكن لَّكُمْ وَأَنتُمْ سكن لَّهُنَّ

They are tranquillity for you, and you are tranquillity for them.[11]

Just as clothes conceal one's private areas, marriage likewise represents a mutual covering of each other's personal blemishes and faults. Just as clothes provide protection from the elements, so do spouses, who protect one another from the difficulties of being single and the difficult seasons of life. Beyond mere protection, clothes offer comfort and beauty to the wearer, and likewise, the comfort that a happy marriage provides is unparalleled. Just as we choose the clothes that will accommodate our needs the most, the mentality of a spouse should be to accommodate and be responsive to the needs of the other. Lastly, seeing that clothes are the closest to us in proximity and exist in direct contact with our skin, spouses ought to maintain closeness to one another and avoid long periods of physical and emotional separation.

3. A miracle in every sense of the word

Marriage involves two individuals who have never known one another, perhaps even having been born and raised in different cultures and climates, suddenly becoming the closest and dearest people to one another in life, sharing a bond of utmost dependency, mercy, and love. Allah ﷻ said:

وَهُوَ الَّذِي خَلَقَ مِنَ الْمَاءِ بَشَرًا فَجَعَلَهُ نَسَبًا وَصِهْرًا وَكَانَ رَبُّكَ قَدِيرًا

And it is He who has created from water a human being and made him [a relative by] lineage and marriage, and your Lord is ever powerful.[12]

---

[11] Al-Ṭabarī, *Tafsīr al-Ṭabarī*.

[12] *Al-Furqān*, 25:54.

4. The most wholesome form of worldly joys

The Prophet ﷺ said:

الدُّنْيَا مَتَاعٌ وَخَيرُ مَتَاعِهَا المَرْأَةُ الصَّالِحَةُ

Life is an enjoyment, and the greatest of its enjoyments is a righteous wife.[13]

Furthermore, when the Prophet ﷺ was asked, "What wealth should we seek to acquire?", his response was different to what they expected, as he said:

لِيَتَّخِذْ أَحَدُكُمْ قَلْبًا شَاكِرًا وَلِسَانًا ذَاكِرًا وَزَوْجَةً مُؤْمِنَةً
تُعِينُ أَحَدَكُمْ عَلَى أَمْرِ الْآخِرَةِ

One of you should seek to acquire a heart which thanks Allah, a tongue which remembers Allah, and a believing wife who will assist you with regard to your Hereafter.[14]

5. Most effective pathway to inner peace

Consider the following verse in which Allah ﷻ declares:

وَمِنْ آيَاتِهِ أَنْ خَلَقَ لَكُمْ مِنْ أَنْفُسِكُمْ أَزْوَاجًا لِتَسْكُنُوا إِلَيْهَا وَجَعَلَ
بَيْنَكُمْ مَوَدَّةً وَرَحْمَةً إِنَّ فِي ذَلِكَ لَآيَاتٍ لِقَوْمٍ يَتَفَكَّرُونَ

And of His signs is that He created for you from yourselves mates that you may find tranquillity in them; and He placed between you affection and mercy. Indeed in that are signs for a people who reflect.

Although these verses are often quoted on wedding invitations, we seldom pay attention to the context of *where* they were revealed in the Qur'an. This is important to consider, because the placement of verses in the Qur'an reveals the importance of that idea relative to other concepts. Consider the following verses:

---

[13] Muslim, *Ṣaḥīḥ Muslim.*

[14] Al-Tirmidhī, *Jāmiʿ al-Tirmidhī.*

وَمِنْ آيَاتِهِ أَنْ خَلَقَكُمْ مِنْ تُرَابٍ ثُمَّ إِذَا أَنْتُمْ بَشَرٌ تَنْتَشِرُونَ

And of His signs is that He created you from dust, then – behold! – you are human beings spreading over the Earth.

وَمِنْ آيَاتِهِ أَنْ خَلَقَ لَكُمْ مِنْ أَنْفُسِكُمْ أَزْوَاجًا لِتَسْكُنُوا إِلَيْهَا وَجَعَلَ
بَيْنَكُمْ مَوَدَّةً وَرَحْمَةً إِنَّ فِي ذَٰلِكَ لَآيَاتٍ لِقَوْمٍ يَتَفَكَّرُونَ

And one of His signs is that He created for you from yourselves mates that you may find tranquillity in them; and He placed between you affection and mercy. Indeed in that are signs for a people who reflect.

وَمِنْ آيَاتِهِ خَلْقُ السَّمَاوَاتِ وَالْأَرْضِ وَاخْتِلَافُ أَلْسِنَتِكُمْ وَأَلْوَانِكُمْ إِنَّ
فِي ذَٰلِكَ لَآيَاتٍ لِلْعَالِمِينَ

And one of His signs is the creation of the Heavens and the Earth, and the diversity of your languages and colours. Surely in this are signs for those of [sound] knowledge.

وَمِنْ آيَاتِهِ مَنَامُكُمْ بِاللَّيْلِ وَالنَّهَارِ وَابْتِغَاؤُكُمْ مِنْ فَضْلِهِ إِنَّ فِي ذَٰلِكَ
لَآيَاتٍ لِقَوْمٍ يَسْمَعُونَ

And one of His signs is your sleep by night and by day for rest as well as your seeking His bounty in both. Surely in this are signs for people who listen.

وَمِنْ آيَاتِهِ يُرِيكُمُ الْبَرْقَ خَوْفًا وَطَمَعًا وَيُنَزِّلُ مِنَ السَّمَاءِ مَاءً فَيُحْيِي بِهِ
الْأَرْضَ بَعْدَ مَوْتِهَا إِنَّ فِي ذَٰلِكَ لَآيَاتٍ لِقَوْمٍ يَعْقِلُونَ

And one of His signs is that He shows you lightning, inspiring [you with] hope and fear. And He sends down rain from the sky, reviving the earth after its death. Surely in this are signs for people who understand.

وَمِنْ آيَاتِهِ أَنْ تَقُومَ السَّمَاءُ وَالْأَرْضُ بِأَمْرِهِ ثُمَّ إِذَا دَعَاكُمْ دَعْوَةً مِنَ
الْأَرْضِ إِذَا أَنْتُمْ تَخْرُجُونَ

And one of His signs is that the Heavens and the Earth persist by His command. Then when He calls you out of the earth just once, you will instantly come forth.[15]

[15] *Al-Rūm*, 30:20-25.

These verses direct our attention to the creation of Allah ﷻ by describing the most awe-inspiring wonders of the universe – humans being created from dust, the stunning variety of our colours and languages, the night and day that govern the cycles of human activity, the electrifying spectacle of lightning, the mercy of the rain that revives a dead earth with lush life-sustaining vegetation and finally – and perhaps most profoundly – how we will all one day emerge from our graves to stand before Him for judgement after He calls us out of the earth "just once".

Among these extraordinary proofs of His Power and Majesty, Allah ﷻ places the seemingly mundane creation of spouses from among humanity. Does this addition seem out of place compared to the might of the other things listed? Perhaps so, for the untrained eye, but the reality is that this union is a phenomenon that holds the same richness and wonder as all the others in their company. The semantic umbrella under which they all reside is no coincidence.

It is also worth noting how Allah ﷻ describes having placed both "affection" and "mercy" between a man and his wife, as the latter usually follows on from the former. Typically, the beginning of relationships will have higher levels of affection than mercy. Then, with the passage of years and with the onset of old-age, illness, and increasing life responsibilities, mutual mercy will reach full maturity. It is this mercy that will ultimately carry the couple through the remainder of the relationship.

Furthermore, love and affection are usually the traits that define relationships between friends, siblings, and the like, whereas mercy usually defines parental relations. So, what then can you say of a relationship that brings together both affection and mercy?

6. A cause for the rise and fall of nations

What goes on within the four walls of your home has a knock-on effect that impacts the entire fabric of society on the greatest level. This is because what we call "society" begins at the smallest possible group: a family. Families live in streets that are neighbourhoods; these neighbourhoods come together to form a town; towns are part of cities; cities form a country. If the unit of the family is broken at its fundamental level, then the repercussions of this will be felt at the highest levels of society. Of all the challenges that threaten the Muslim Ummah locally and globally, the disintegration of the Muslim family is one of the most threatening realities. Many of the deeper travesties and traumas that plague humanity can arguably be traced back to dysfunction within the family unit.

This is not an alarmist assessment, but one rooted in clear social research and historical precedent.

In a momentous historical study, Edward Gibbon, one of the world's greatest historians, identified five main causes of the decline and fall of Roman civilisation, which were:

1. The weakening sense of individual responsibility
2. The breakdown of the family structure
3. Seeking pleasures that became increasingly hedonistic, violent, and immoral
4. Excessive taxes, government control, and intervention
5. The decline of religion.

7. A topic that Shayṭān has given abundant attention

Whilst many of us belittle the significance of such a discussion, Shayṭān – along with his allies who invest endless time and effort into dismantling the family unit – understand that their success in breaking up a home constitutes one of the greatest triumphs.

The Prophet ﷺ said:

إِنَّ إِبْلِيسَ يَضَعُ عَرْشَهُ عَلَى الْمَاءِ ثُمَّ يَبْعَثُ سَرَايَاهُ فَأَدْنَاهُمْ مِنْهُ مَنْزِلَةً أَعْظَمُهُمْ فِتْنَةً، يَجِيءُ أَحَدُهُمْ فَيَقُولُ: فَعَلْتُ كَذَا وَكَذَا، فَيَقُولُ: مَا صَنَعْتَ شَيْئًا، قَالَ ثُمَّ يَجِيءُ أَحَدُهُمْ فَيَقُولُ: مَا تَرَكْتُهُ حَتَّى فَرَّقْتُ بَيْنَهُ وَبَيْنَ امْرَأَتِهِ، قَالَ: فَيُدْنِيهِ مِنْهُ وَيَقُولُ: نِعْمَ أَنْتَ

> Iblīs places his throne over the water and then he sends out his troops. The nearest to him are the greatest at causing *fitnah*. One of them says, "I have done this and this." Iblīs says, "You have done nothing." Another says, "I did not leave this person until I separated between him and his wife." Iblīs says, "You have done well."[16]

Why is this? Because he is fully aware of the severe repercussions that often follow divorce. There are a plethora of harms that hurt the entire family on an individual, emotional, mental, practical and spiritual level. These consequences are felt dramatically in the short-term, but also continue to impact family members well into the future. Research demonstrating a correlation between life traumas (such as divorce) and poor mental and physical health, emotional dysfunction, insecurity around relationships and insecure attachments within the family is readily available.

The sad reality of our times is that, with soaring rates of divorce and single parent homes, children today are now more likely to have a smartphone than a father at home. Surprisingly,

[16] Muslim, *Ṣaḥīḥ Muslim*.

research even links divorce to increased rates of child obesity, because less time and money is likely to be invested into serving regular, nutritious meals for children. Parents are also likely to overfeed their family, and children often rely on emotional eating (largely consuming processed, high-fat, high-sugar foods) as an emotional coping mechanism for the stress of handling the separation. If current trends remain as they are, a child born today in the UK has more than a one-in-three chance of not living with both birth parents by the age of 15.[17]

Rising divorce rates have now become a global phenomenon in spite of geographical and religious variances – marriages are breaking down in the East, the Global South and the West alike.

For the 2.4 million US couples who will marry this year, 43% of their marriages are not expected to survive. This is not a phenomenon only in the "West", as similar statistics are present in the Muslim world, which has seen dramatic increases in divorce rates. In some parts of Saudi Arabia, 60% of marriages end in divorce, while divorce rates in the Gulf Coast Country hit an all-time high of 70% in countries like Qatar. In Egypt, a divorce takes place every two minutes. Similarly, divorce rates have surged in China, where 4.2 million divorces heralded an 8.3% increase on the year before.

Across the world, statistics regarding marital breakdowns are both alarming and sadly consistent. According to the noted Princeton University family historian Lawrence Stone, "The scale of marital breakdowns in the West since the year 1960 has no historical precedent that I know of, and seems unique – there has been nothing like it for the last 2000 years, and probably longer."

---

[17] "Top Ten Key Facts on Marriage." Marriage Foundation. November 25, 2023. https://marriagefoundation.org.uk/top-ten-key-facts-on-marriage/

It is no exaggeration to say that a tsunami of family breakdowns is battering the entire globe.

Clearly, something is wrong on a deeper level. To try to reverse this worrying trend, various initiatives have been put in place by governments: we now see marriage grants, group weddings, dowry-caps and even divorce exams and penalties put into action to stem the tide of family breakdown. However, these interventions can only have limited impact without addressing the root causes of marital breakdown.

The human heart is a vessel that has been created for the worship, glorification, and adoration of Allah ﷻ. If this vessel is instead filled with the burdens and sorrows of marital disputes, then the truest manifestations of inner fatigue manifest, replacing the intended tranquillity of marriage with restlessness, traction with distraction, and happiness with grief. The consequences of this ordeal extend like tentacles, constricting one's career, social life, community life, and, most importantly, spiritual progress. No food, sport or outings can do away with the lingering pain, leaving one at the mercy of the Most Merciful. How true are the words of Allah ﷻ:

وَخُلِقَ ٱلْإِنسَـٰنُ ضَعِيفًا

And man was created weak.[18]

So, bearing in mind this weak nature of ours, how times have changed, how important a stable household is to every form of wellbeing, the rising rates of divorce, and Shayṭān's endless pursuit of dismantling families, we must respond in a way that is equal to the immense challenge before us through an honest and holistic retreat to the Book of Allah ﷻ.

[18] *Al-Nisā'*, 4:28.

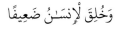

Allah ﷻ said:

وَكُلَّ شَيْءٍ فَصَّلْنَاهُ تَفْصِيلًا

And everything We have set out in detail.[19]

He ﷻ also said:

وَلَقَدْ جِئْنَاهُمْ بِكِتَابٍ فَصَّلْنَاهُ عَلَىٰ عِلْمٍ

Certainly, We have brought them a Book which We have explained in detail with knowledge.[20]

The Qur'an also declares that:

مَا كَانَ حَدِيثًا يُفْتَرَىٰ وَلَـٰكِن تَصْدِيقَ الَّذِي بَيْنَ يَدَيْهِ وَتَفْصِيلَ كُلِّ شَيْءٍ
وَهُدًى وَرَحْمَةً لِّقَوْمٍ يُؤْمِنُونَ

Never was the Qur'an a narration invented, but a confirmation of what was before it and a detailed explanation of all things, and guidance and mercy for a people who believe.[21]

Considering this, the 20 Qur'anic principles on which this book rests are universal (apply everywhere), timeless, and self-evident (their wisdom is immediately apparent to a balanced and fair human being). All the principles within this book are just as true in the world of human relations as the law of gravity is in the physical world.

With that said, let us begin our journey!

---

[19] *Al-Isrā'*, 17:12.
[20] *Al-A'rāf*, 7:52.
[21] *Yūsuf*, 12:111.

CHAPTER ONE

On setting intentions

وَمَا خَلَقْتُ الْجِنَّ وَالْإِنسَ إِلَّا لِيَعْبُدُونِ

And I did not create the jinn and man except so that they may worship Me.[22]

For many believers, this verse of the Qur'an may be quite familiar. It is one that is often cited in response to questions surrounding the purpose of life. "Why are we here?" "Why did Allah create me?" "What is the meaning of life?", and other similar questions are often answered with this simple, unambiguous, and profound statement. Why then would this verse be applicable in discussions of marriage?

The connection between two people within marriage and the worship of Allah ﷻ may not appear obvious at first. However, to truly understand the correct approach to marriage, we must explore (and, if necessary, correct) our concept of worship first.

In the life of any believer, there is no principle more important and central than worship. Every intention, statement, and action we make can and must be traced back to this concept. Images of mosques, prayer mats, and the recitation of the Qur'an come to mind when we think of "worship". The reality of this concept, however, is something much more expansive,

[22] *Al-Dhāriyāt*, 51:56.

holistic, and inclusive than this. To understand the true nature of worship in Islam is a transformative act that will give you the power to live life in an entirely different way.

To begin with definitions, the concept of worship within Islam (*ʿibādah*) is of two types:

1. *Khāṣṣah* (specific or listed acts), such as the five pillars of Islam and what branches out from them. These are prescribed actions that are heavily regulated by the Shariah.
2. *ʿĀmmah* (general, or unlisted acts), which pertains to *all* aspects of life, including practical acts such as eating, drinking, and sleeping. These are regulated in a lighter manner by the Shariah.

ʿIbādah therefore is a vast umbrella term that canopies over every aspect of life, as Allah's book indicates:

قُلْ إِنَّ صَلَاتِي وَنُسُكِي وَمَحْيَايَ وَمَمَاتِي لِلَّهِ رَبِّ الْعَالَمِينَ

Say, "Surely my prayer, my worship, my life, and my death are all for Allah – Lord of all worlds."[23]

Today, many are guilty of conceiving *ʿibādah* only within the narrow confines of prescribed acts of worship relegated to particular times, places and settings. The reality, however, is that for a believer, *ʿibādah* is a holistic state of being that encompasses our entire life. Let us look at what the scholars of our tradition understood worship to be.

Imam Ibn Taymiyyah ﵀ said:

الْعِبَادَةَ هِيَ اسْم جَامع لكل مَا يُحِبهُ الله ويرضاه من الْأَقْوَال والأعمال الْبَاطِنَة وَالظَّاهِرَة

[23] *Al-Anʿām*, 6:162.

> *'Ibādah* is a comprehensive term that covers every matter that is beloved to Allah and pleasing to Him, whether verbal or physical, and whether outward or inward.[24]

For a matter so vast and all-encompassing, how can we be sure that our thoughts, speech, and actions actually fall within the definition of "worship" in Islam? We are given a clear and concise criterion to judge this, as any deed can be considered worship as long as it fulfils the following two conditions:

- Sincerity (performing the deed only for Allah's Pleasure)
- Compliance with the Prophetic Sunnah

Immediately, our conception of worship is radically altered by adopting this approach within our lives. If any mere *thought* can be counted as an act of worship, then what can be said for the life-changing, public, and long-term event of marriage, which merges the lives of two people together as long as they live?

Marriage must be seen in the same light of worship as all our other actions for His sake. It is something that can and should be done firstly for the sake of Allah ﷻ, and secondly in line with the Prophetic Sunnah. This means that those who honour it are fulfilling part of their purpose of life and increasing their chance of attaining Paradise, while those who do not are neglecting part of their purpose of life and are therefore jeopardising their entry into the eternal abode.

Marriage is not just a rite of passage, a brief, joyful day after which two people are left to their own devices to figure out what to do with life. Rather, it is such a profoundly important union that the Divine law of Allah ﷻ – the Shariah – has directly regulated many aspects of marriage to ensure it is carried out in the best of ways.

[24] Ibn Taymiyyah, *Kitāb al-'Ubūdiyyah*.

Examples of this regulation include stipulations ensuring that women are consulted before marriage:

لاَ تُنْكَحُ الأَيِّمُ حَتَّى تُسْتَأْمَرَ وَلاَ تُنْكَحُ الْبِكْرُ حَتَّى تُسْتَأْذَنَ

An unmarried woman should not be given in marriage except after consulting her, and a virgin should not be given in marriage except after her permission.[25]

As well as guidelines for the proposal process:

لَا يَخْطُبَ الرَّجُلُ عَلَى خِطْبَةِ أَخِيهِ حَتَّى يَتْرُكَ الْخَاطِبُ
قَبْلَهُ أَوْ يَأْذَنَ لَهُ الْخَاطِبُ

No one of you should ask a woman in marriage when his brother has done so already, until the one who has proposed [to her] before him gives her up or gives him permission.[26]

And guidelines in the event of a marriage:

لَا نِكَاحَ إِلَّا بِوَلِيٍّ وَشَاهِدَيْ عَدْلٍ

There is no marriage except with a guardian and two credible witnesses.[27]

And guidelines for the event of divorce:

يَـٰٓأَيُّهَا لنَّبِيُّ إِذَا طَلَّقْتُمُ لنِّسَآءَ فَطَلِّقُوهُنَّ لِعِدَّتِهِنَّ وَأَحْصُوا لْعِدَّةَ وَتَّقُوا
للَّهَ رَبَّكُمْ لَا تُخْرِجُوهُنَّ مِن بُيُوتِهِنَّ وَلَا يَخْرُجْنَ إِلَّآ أَن يَأْتِينَ بِفَـٰحِشَةٍ
مُّبَيِّنَةٍ وَتِلْكَ حُدُودُ للَّهِ وَمَن يَتَعَدَّ حُدُودَ للَّهِ فَقَدْ ظَلَمَ نَفْسَهُ لَا تَدْرِى
لَعَلَّ للَّهَ يُحْدِثُ بَعْدَ ذَٰلِكَ أَمْرًا

O Prophet! Instruct the believers: "When you intend to divorce women, then divorce them during their waiting period, and count it accurately. And fear Allah, your Lord. Do not force them out of their homes, nor should they leave – unless they commit a blatant misconduct. These are the limits set by Allah.

---

[25] Al-Bukhārī, *Ṣaḥīḥ al-Bukhārī.*

[26] Al-Bukhārī, *Ṣaḥīḥ al-Bukhārī;* Muslim, *Ṣaḥīḥ Muslim.*

[27] Al-Bayhaqī, *Al-Sunan al-Kubrā li al-Bayhaqī.*

And whoever transgresses Allah's limits has truly wronged his own soul. You never know – perhaps Allah will bring about a change of heart later."[28]

As well as these stipulations, there are careful instructions for many other aspects of marriage and divorce including intimacy, custody of children, and financial arrangements. The care within these guidelines indicate beyond any doubt that the act of marriage is to be seen as an integral and esteemed form of worship.

What changes when you view marriage as worship?

1. None of your marital challenges and joys go to waste

Whether you have the correct intention or not, marriage is going to present you with highs, lows, troubles, and sacrifices. This is a universal reality for both those who have faith and those without a belief system. So since you have already signed up for an eventful journey ahead, why not align your intention first so that the same actions you would have otherwise been doing become a source of divine reward for you? Without such an intention, your efforts are much like a labourer who works long hours for free, when they could have been rewarded for all their efforts.

In practical terms, seeing your marriage as worship means that money you spend on the household counts as charity, acts of kindness towards your spouse and children earn divine pleasure, and even the act of intimacy you enjoy brings you reward from Allah ﷻ. Conversely, your struggle within marriage becomes something you can grow from, and life's inevitable challenges are seen as part of a grand plan for your life.

[28] *Al-Ṭalāq*, 65:1.

Ibn Abī Jamrah ﷺ said:

وَدِدْتُ أَنَّهُ لَوْ كَانَ مِنْ الْفُقَهَاءِ مَنْ لَيْسَ لَهُ شُغْلٌ إِلَّا أَنْ يُعَلِّمَ النَّاسَ مَقَاصِدَهُمْ فِي أَعْمَالِهِمْ وَيَقْعُدَ إِلَى التَّدْرِيسِ فِي أَعْمَالِ النِّيَّاتِ لَيْسَ إِلَّا أَوْ كَلَامًا هَذَا مَعْنَاهُ فَإِنَّهُ مَا أَتَى عَلَى كَثِيرٍ مِنْ النَّاسِ إِلَّا مِنْ تَضْيِيعِ النِّيَّاتِ

I wish that some of the scholars of Islam would devote their entire time to teaching people the art of intention setting for their actions, such that scholars would sit and educate people in this regard without doing anything else. This is because many people fall into ruin for no reason other than falling short in their intentions.[29]

Many of us suffer so much throughout the course of our marriages because of a weak or absent intention.

Regarding this, some of the scholars of Islam have said:

عِبَادَاتُ أَهْلِ الغَفْلَةِ عَادَاتٌ وَعَادَاتُ أَهْلِ اليَقَظَةِ عِبَادَاتٌ

The worship of the absent-minded are habits, and the habits of the present-minded are worship.

When you view marriage as *ʿibādah*, everything you do and experience during that marriage is transformed into an opportunity to gain reward. Your difficulties also become a means through which you expiate sins and heal shortcomings. This is apparent in the following Hadith:

دِينَارٌ أَنْفَقْتَهُ فِي سَبِيلِ اللهِ وَدِينَارٌ أَنْفَقْتَهُ فِي رَقَبَةٍ وَدِينَارٌ تَصَدَّقْتَ بِهِ عَلَى مِسْكِينٍ وَدِينَارٌ أَنْفَقْتَهُ عَلَى أَهْلِكَ أَعْظَمُهَا أَجْرًا الَّذِي أَنْفَقْتَهُ عَلَى أَهْلِكَ

A dinar you spend in Allah's way, or to free a slave, or as a charity you give to a needy person, or to support your family, the one yielding the greatest reward is that which you spend on your family.[30]

---

[29] *Al-Madkhal.*

[30] Muslim, *Ṣaḥīḥ Muslim.*

The Prophet ﷺ also said:

إِنَّكَ لَنْ تُنْفِقَ نَفَقَةً تَبْتَغِي بِهَا وَجْهَ اللَّهِ إِلَّا أُجِرْتَ
عَلَيْهَا حَتَّى مَا تَجْعَلُ فِي فَمِ امْرَأَتِكَ

You will be rewarded for whatever you spend for Allah's sake even if it were a morsel which you put in your wife's mouth.[31]

Incredibly, the Messenger of Allah ﷺ also informed us that:

وفي بُضْعِ أَحَدِكُمْ صَدَقَةٌ، قالوا: يا رَسولَ اللهِ، أَيَأتي أَحَدُنَا شَهْوَتَهُ
وَيَكونُ له فِيهَا أَجْرٌ؟ قالَ: أَرَأَيْتُمْ لو وَضَعَهَا في حَرَامٍ، أَكانَ عليه فِيهَا
وِزْرٌ؟ فَكَذلكَ إِذَا وَضَعَهَا في الحَلَالِ كانَ له أَجْرٌ

"Your intimate moments with your spouse are an act of charity." The Companions asked, "O Messenger of Allah, can it be that we get rewarded for acting upon our desires?" He responded, "Is it not true that if one had fulfilled his desire in a prohibited manner, he would be sinful? So likewise, fulfilling it in a permissible way brings about reward."[32]

However, the view that sexual love is a kind of evil was prevalent in Christian discussions of marriage within the Church until the Reformation of the sixteenth century. The early church fathers Tertullian and Ambrose preferred the extinction of mankind to its propagation through sex. Another church father, Origen, had himself castrated before his ordination as a form of devotion. In contrast to this, Islam's understanding of sexual love is that it is a tender act of worship that is accepted by Allah ﷻ when within the safe parameters of marriage.

---

[31] Al-Bukhārī, *Ṣaḥīḥ al-Bukhārī*.

[32] Muslim, *Ṣaḥīḥ Muslim*.

2. You will unlock an immense store of patience

When marriage is seen through a lens of worship, new horizons of patience open up, as you have elevated your perspective on this relationship from regarding it as mundane to something divine. Why is this particularly important? Because every phase of marriage requires patience. Some obvious examples include the patience required during the months (or years) searching for a spouse and the patience required to endure rejection. Likewise, the fiscal patience required to face a mahr (dowry) that is unaffordable and the difficulty of providing as a breadwinner that follows, as well as the emotional patience required to endure drifting apart or falling out of love is yet more difficult, especially when the complexities of intimacy and differences in libido are involved. The influence of family and clashes between your wife and mother require patience to navigate, particularly when living under a single roof. You must have the patience to lose a battle in order to win a war, especially as a parent who has a duty to preserve your spouse's honour in the eyes of your children. The bleaker moments of life, including financial strain, fertility issues, the death of loved ones, and even the breakdown of marriage, all require an incredible degree of patience to endure and remain committed to Islamic morality.

These are but a few of the inexhaustible situations in married life when you must rely on patience. To foster this indispensable trait, we must view marriage as an act of worship that demands the highest ethics in us. In this way, you will be successful in building something far greater than a household in this life; you shall be constructing a home in the Hereafter and making a case for Allah ﷻ to accept all your deeds.

Putting this principle into practice

1. Always revisit and renew intentions

Expect the reward of Allah ﷻ in all that you do during your married life – this is called having *iḥtisāb*. "I have paid the rent" – *iḥtisāb*. "I cleaned the home" – *iḥtisāb*. "I cooked a meal for my family" – *iḥtisāb*. "I pleased my spouse with marital relations" – *iḥtisāb*. When your intentions are to please Allah ﷻ, all actions become worship.

2. Display visual aids for regular reminders

This could be on your fridge, in your home office, bedroom, or anywhere you would notice. Phrase the reminder of *iḥtisāb* as you wish – it could be a Hadith on intentions or a verse from the Qur'an that you connect with strongly. Your environment can help remind you that your marriage is worship in times of forgetfulness or heightened emotions.

3. Gather your family to learn and bond together

Take the lead in setting an example within the home through regular group studies of the Qur'an, Sunnah, *sīrah* (prophetic biography) and their likes, doing so in an age-appropriate way if children are participating. This simple effort will keep your marriage connected to Heaven, helping you focus on matters that transcend the earthly bond and remind you of something far greater.

CHAPTER TWO

On aligning perspectives

وَأَخَذْنَ مِنكُم مِّيثَاقًا غَلِيظًا

And they (your wives) have taken from you a firm covenant.[33]

This principle is not entirely about what you do outwardly, but how to foster an internal shift in perspective before embarking on the journey of marriage. Marriage is perhaps the most legally significant thing you will do, other than having children or dying, as it radically changes your rights and obligations. The wedding may be the day of beautiful clothing, friends and family celebrating and cutting a big cake, but marriage is something else entirely. The nikāḥ is simply, yet profoundly, a legally binding contract and a solemn covenant although the formal process takes but a few seconds. The simplicity of the nikāḥ, however, does not take away from its gravity and weight. As soon as the nikāḥ is complete, hundreds of rulings are in place between those two people who were Islamically – before that moment – perfect strangers.

What do the words "a firm covenant" evoke in your mind? To get a sense of the gravity of marriage in Islam, let us examine

[33] *Al-Nisā'*, 4:21.

how it is used in the Book of Allah ﷻ. In the entire Qur'an, this strong expression of "a firm covenant" has only been used in reference to three matters:

1. The covenant which Allah ﷻ took from the followers of Moses ﷺ, when He said:

وَقُلْنَا لَهُمْ لَا تَعْدُوا فِي السَّبْتِ وَأَخَذْنَا مِنْهُمْ مِيثَاقًا غَلِيظًا

And We said to them, "Do not transgress on the Sabbath", and We took from them a firm covenant![34]

2. The covenant which Allah ﷻ took from the Prophets ﷺ, when He said:

وَإِذْ أَخَذْنَا مِنَ النَّبِيِّينَ مِيثَاقَهُمْ وَمِنْكَ وَمِنْ نُوحٍ وَإِبْرَاهِيمَ وَمُوسَى
وَعِيسَى ابْنِ مَرْيَمَ وَأَخَذْنَا مِنْهُمْ مِيثَاقًا غَلِيظًا

And when We made a covenant with the Prophets and with you, and with Nūḥ, Ibrāhīm, Mūsā, and ʿIsā son of Maryam, and We made with them a firm covenant.[35]

3: The covenant between man and his wife, when He said:

وَكَيْفَ تَأْخُذُونَهُ وَقَدْ أَفْضَى بَعْضُكُمْ إِلَى
بَعْضٍ وَأَخَذْنَ مِنْكُمْ مِيثَاقًا غَلِيظًا

And how could you take it back after having enjoyed each other intimately and she has taken from you a firm covenant?[36]

To give just a few examples which illustrate the magnitude of this "firm covenant", consider the following narrations.

With regards to one's wife, the Prophet ﷺ said:

---

[34] *Al-Nisā'*, 4:154.
[35] *Al-Aḥzāb*, 33:7.
[36] *Al-Nisā', 4:21.*

اللَّهُمَّ إِنِّي أُحَرِّجُ حَقَّ الضَّعِيفَيْنِ: الْيَتِيمِ وَالْمَرْأَةِ

O Allah! I declare it very sinful should the rights of the two weak ones not be safeguarded; the orphans and women.[37]

Similarly, with regards to one's husband, the aunt of the Companion al-Ḥuṣayn ibn Miḥṣan ﵁ once approached the Prophet ﷺ with a matter that she required assistance with. After having helped her, the Prophet ﷺ asked her, "Are you married?", she said, "Yes." He asked her, "How do you behave with him?", She said, "I do not prevent him from anything which he requests, except those matters that I cannot fulfil." He ﷺ then said to her:

فَانْظُرِي أَيْنَ أَنْتِ مِنْهُ، فَإِنَّمَا هُوَ جَنَّتُكِ وَنَارُكِ

Ensure that you carefully observe how you are with him, for he is your Paradise or Hellfire.[38]

When Muʿādh ibn Jabal ﵁ returned back to Medina from al-Shām, he prostrated to the Prophet ﷺ. The Prophet ﷺ said, "O Muʿādh, what is this?" He replied, "I have come to you from al-Shām, where they prostrate to their patriarchs and bishops, and so I wished that we do the same for you."

He ﷺ said:

فَلَا تَفْعَلُوا ؛ فَإِنِّي لَوْ كُنْتُ آمِرًا أَحَدًا أَنْ يَسْجُدَ لِغَيْرِ اللَّهِ ، لَأَمَرْتُ الْمَرْأَةَ أَنْ تَسْجُدَ لِزَوْجِهَا

Do not do that. But if I were to instruct someone to prostrate to other than Allah, I would have instructed wives to prostrate to their husbands.[39]

Even a glance at such narrations, without studying the mutual rights and obligations spouses hold between one another, makes it clear that marriage is in fact a relationship like none other.

---

[37] Al-Nasāʾī, *Al-Sunan al-Ṣughrā li al-Nasāʾī.*
[38] Ibn Ḥanbal, *Musnad Aḥmad.*
[39] Ibn Mājah, *Sunan Ibn Mājah.*

In today's world, marriage is often no longer seen or treated as a covenant or a life-long commitment. It is simply a contract between consenting adults – one that is oftentimes considered unnecessary and is easily broken when no longer seen as convenient. Marital contracts are often drawn up in anticipation of possible failure through a prenuptial agreement. Society and God are no longer taken into consideration. The legal system has softened conditions on divorce, making it ever more accessible, quicker, and cheaper.

Why do we find such a dismissive approach towards marriage today?

1. The normalisation of extramarital relationships

In an era where multiple sexual relationships have become the norm, the success of long-term marriages has been severely impacted. At the Institute for Family Studies, Professor Nicholas Wolfinger, a sociologist at the University of Utah, has found that Americans who have only ever slept with their spouses are most likely to report being in a "very happy" marriage. Meanwhile, the lowest odds of marital happiness belong to women who have had six to ten sexual partners in their lives. For men, there is still a dip in marital satisfaction after one partner, but it is never as low as it gets for women. Professor Wolfinger states, "Perhaps it is not unexpected that having many partners increases the odds of divorce."

"Those who have never had sex with anyone but their spouse may be the kind of people who value commitment highly," said Andrew Cherlin, a Johns Hopkins University sociologist. "They have never been interested in sex without commitment, and once married, they may be more committed to their spouses, and therefore happier."

To separate sexual relationships from the commitment of marriage has led not only to a decrease in the number of people choosing to marry, but also in lower rates of marital satisfaction once they do.

2. Influence from feminist discourse

Both early and contemporary feminist thinkers often herald marriage as an institution that primarily serves patriarchy and oppresses women. Marriage is seen as an unnecessary social construct designed to benefit men, offering few redeeming features for women. Sheila Cronan claimed that the freedom for women "cannot be won without the abolition of marriage." Marlene Dixon of the Democratic Workers Party wrote that "The institution of marriage is the chief vehicle for the perpetuation of the oppression of women; it is through the role of 'wife' that the subjugation of women is maintained." In the book "The Second Sex", the philosopher Simone de Beauvoir argues that marriage is an alienating institution and called for the dismantling of the nuclear family. Much of this discourse – which is a reaction to historical, legal and social injustices when it comes to weddings, family life, and divorce – has gained traction even within Muslim communities.

3. Satire that trivialises the gravity of marriage

We live in a culture where few things are beyond the reach of satire and mockery. This attitude towards marriage has trickled down to the "dinner table test" and common daily conversations where a person's spouse is seen as fair game to make fun of. The nature of this humour can quickly turn sarcastic, mocking, and demeaning. In fact, married people often make jokes at the expense of their partners to the point where the comedic trope of marriage is two people who hate one another. This form of humour is often dubbed harmless, but it has a real impact on relationships and people.

In fact, even children will often go around declaring they will *never* get married. Why do they announce this intention to everyone? Have six-year-olds somehow absorbed radical feminist notions of marriage being a tool of patriarchy? Have they scrutinised the balance of rights and responsibilities in marriage before they came to their conclusion? Of course not. Primarily, children appear to be reacting against the notion of marriage simply based on the observations of married people around them, deciding that it is not the kind of situation they want to end up in if they can avoid it.

How did we end up here? Many caricatures and cheap jokes at the expense of marriage have been normalised via the vehicle of satire. Marriage is a ball and chain. Men make jokes about how they cannot do anything in life without permission from their wives, and how much these same wives do nothing more than endlessly talk and pursue shopping addictions.

Women make jokes about how men do not listen, are incompetent, and unavailable to their families. The classic one is about how boring or unexciting spouses are to one another, and how we are so excited to plan activities without them for some fun and freedom away from the "mister" or "missus".

Men make jokes about how dull their wives are because they do not like cricket, and women infantilise men by equating them with their children. These jokes do not just insult the people in the relationship, they are also reductive in their stereotyping of gender roles, commitment, and marriage. Being in a relationship that is subject to even this seemingly innocuous social ridicule can be very damaging, especially for women, who are constantly bombarded by society with the idea that being a homemaker is a failed outcome lacking worth, value, or ambition.

While marriage is mercilessly mocked, alternative lifestyles of "liberated" promiscuity, same-sex relationship "experiments", and "no strings" relationships are presented as exciting, fresh, and socially acceptable alternatives. Relationships are treated just as disposable as fast-food packaging, consumed and thrown out without a second thought. Marriage, on the other hand, is seen as an unnecessary, complicated, and oppressive institution. The framing of marriage must be interrogated as the negative messaging has an undeniable consequence on even the Muslim psyche.

Though many may defend such humour as harmless banter, we ought to be conscious of the words we utter and the consequences they may have. Marriage is something divinely sanctified and worth defending the importance of. There is a context, time, and place for everything within Islam and humour absolutely has a place between spouses within the safety and privacy of a loving relationship – where jokes are made that lighten the mood, bond, and bring two people even closer together. This is entirely different from tasteless jokes made in public spaces, which are open to misinterpretation and cause offence or invite ridicule against your spouse.

There is an array of grave consequences when the matter of marriage is trivialised in society. These include, but are not limited to:

- Secret marriages taking place against all the regular vetting procedures and without the knowledge, safeguarding procedures, or consent of family. Often such marriages are conducted with the intention to divorce, or at least a strong openness to it.
- Not knowing the mutual rights of one another. When people do not consider marriage as an important sacred union, they do not expend even the most basic effort to

learn about the distinct roles and responsibilities required of them in the partnership.

- Lack of tolerance between the spouses, including how casually the word "divorce" is thrown around during heated exchanges. The increasing rates of husbands issuing ṭalāq and wives instigating khulʿ speaks to how marriage has lost its sanctity, even for married couples.

- Some Shariah councils themselves have developed a relaxed attitude to separating husband and wife. In some cases, neither of the parties meet, reconciliation is not even attempted, and no face-to-face meetings are even suggested. A heavy matter like divorce deserves care and time, as the marital bond being broken is a "firm covenant" torn apart.

- Interfering in a marriage to weaken it. A "humorous" warning that has been given to men is to "be careful of your wife's friends, as they are the management committee of your marriage" says what you need to know about how over-sharing private details of your marriage can lead to disastrous outcomes. As such, advice should only be sought from those who understand that they are dealing with a "firm covenant" between two people. Consider the following Hadith:

لَيْسَ مِنَّا مَنْ خَبَّبَ امْرَأَةً عَلَى زَوْجِهَا

Anyone who incites a woman against
her husband is not one of us.[40]

Far from being a trivial matter and the subject of idle gossip, marriage is a bond so strong that interfering in it brings about consequences as severe as the disavowal of the Prophet ﷺ.

[40] Abū Dāwūd, *Sunan Abū Dāwūd.*

Putting this principle into practice

The first step to reviving the idea of marriage as a "firm covenant" is to spread awareness of this concept within your circles of influence, whether that is from parents to children, teachers to students, or elders to young couples. This principle is about an internal realignment to treat marriage with the respect it deserves in the face of ideologies and cultural attitudes that devalue it entirely.

On an individual level, make a commitment to yourself to complete the study of these chapters as an expression of your desire to preserve the sanctity of marriage. Encourage friends and family to do the same until this concept is revered as it deserves to be.

Lastly, put an end to all forms of mockery pertaining to marriage and call out this behaviour when you hear it. Draw people's attention to the consequences of using marriage as comedic relief and how we have become – as a society – desensitised to this. This does not mean being the party-pooper among friends, but being the one who, with confidence and wisdom, draws the community to a higher ideal.

CHAPTER THREE

On selecting criteria

وَأَنْكِحُوا الْأَيَامَىٰ مِنْكُمْ وَالصَّالِحِينَ مِنْ عِبَادِكُمْ وَإِمَائِكُمْ

Give in marriage the free singles among you, as well as the righteous of your bondmen and bondwomen.[41]

Marriage is a lifelong journey that involves making many difficult decisions along the way. All humans make decisions based on their values, and the more shared values you have, the smoother your partnership will be. Staying aligned on shared religious values is critical when establishing a household together. The many practical areas of life will involve having mutual goals in mind – from establishing prayer in the home, educating your children, preparing for hajj or *ʿumrah*, and choosing a career to pursue.

These are some of the key decisions you will find yourselves needing to navigate together, well after the initial honeymoon period of the early months or years of the marriage have settled. In the humdrum of life's responsibilities, the contentment of your daily routine will depend on how compatible you are in your shared outlook. As such, striving to become righteous and searching for a spouse on the same path is a critical part of your search for a life partner.

[41] *Al-Nūr*, 24:32.

Let us explore the two most famous narrations in this regard.

The Prophet ﷺ said:

تُنْكَحُ المَرْأَةُ لأَرْبَعٍ: لِمَالِهَا وَلِحَسَبِهَا وَلِجَمَالِهَا وَلِدِينِهَا
فَاظْفَرْ بِذَاتِ الدِّينِ تَرِبَتْ يَدَاكَ

Women are usually married for their wealth, lineage, beauty, and dīn (i.e., religious commitment), so seize the religiously committed one so that may you prosper.[42]

Let us look at each of these qualities in turn:

1. Wealth

Though it may not be popular to say, wealthy people often tend to want to marry wealthy people, sometimes to preserve social standing, but also to have their child's standard of living maintained at the same level after marriage. Indeed, the Shariah encourages people to search for a spouse who shares a similar socio-economic background, as this eases many practical issues of lifestyle post-marriage. Although many people may not realise the significance of this when they enter into a love-struck marriage, such differences in background can and do crop up later on in life.

2. Lineage

There are two concepts in Arabic: nasab and ḥasab. As for nasab, this is lineage with respect to who you descend from. Some communities are more aware of their lineages than others and are able to trace it back many generations. So, marrying outside of that clan into a family who do not give the same importance to genealogy is, to them, problematic. As for ḥasab, this is what our ancestors have done to distinguish them,

[42] Al-Bukhārī, *Ṣaḥīḥ al-Bukhārī*; Muslim, *Ṣaḥīḥ Muslim*.

such that to be the descendant of a king or a warrior is part of one's ḥasab and imparts a distinguished standing compared to others. Hearts, by their nature, are traditionally inclined towards being part of a noble heritage. So, some people marry from certain families to create a link to an honoured individual or family.

3. Beauty

Beauty is a universally appealing trait, and our inclination towards it is part of our *fiṭrah*. However, we often get desensitised to what we see on a daily basis, and the novelty of our initial attraction may fade. The most beautiful looking people can look really bad on their bad days. The face is, by its nature, very malleable, and can often surprise you with how different it can look in different scenarios. The natural passage of time affects perceptions of conventional beauty, as you will inevitably witness your spouse start to age. People may also be affected with an illness that alters their appearance or suffer an accident that does the same. If the purpose of that marriage was solely hinged on aesthetics, then when that aspect begins to change – as it inevitably will – then what do you have left in your marriage that is lasting and secure?

4. Religion

How interesting it is that the last of the four qualities mentioned in the Hadith is religion. This itself explains so much in the messy landscape of today's marriages, as it is a quality sorely lacking. For this reason, the words used in the conclusion of the Hadith are noteworthy: the Prophet ﷺ did not say "tazawwaj" (marry) or "ikhtar" (choose), but instead said "faẓfar bi dhāt al-dīn." The term "iẓfar" literally refers to the seizing of a prize, snatching it out of the hands of competitors, and getting to it first. It is as if the Prophet ﷺ is saying, "that which people have placed at the end of their list, you should place at the very top of yours." Indeed, religion outlives everything else and continues to shine brightest even in life's darkest hours. The phrasing of this quality is a tacit encouragement towards people that such a quality of religion is rare, valuable, and should never be passed by. The quality of strong dīn in a person is not subject to depreciation or regret, as can happen with a wealthy person, a very beautiful spouse, or a person of strong lineage but poor character. Of all qualities, firm religious commitment provides the most solid ground on which to walk the path of marriage.

The second narration is as follows:

إِذَا خَطَبَ إِلَيْكُمْ مَنْ تَرْضَوْنَ دِينَهُ وَخُلُقَهُ فَزَوِّجُوهُ، إِلَّا تَفْعَلُوا تَكُنْ فِتْنَةٌ فِي الأَرْضِ ، وَفَسَادٌ عَرِيضٌ

If you are approached by a person of good dīn and character who wishes to marry your daughter, then marry him to her. If you do not, there will be tribulation on the land and widespread corruption.[43]

Notice the additional criteria of "khuluq" (character) mentioned when choosing a husband that was not included in the Hadith about choosing a wife. Perhaps the wisdom for this is that women are, in most marriages, in a position of greater vulnerability than men, and therefore there is a greater additional emphasis on khuluq to safeguard her interests. Indeed, how "good" is a so-called "religious" man who is – for example – easily angered, stingy, negligent, or heavy-handed towards his wife?

These two narrations are at the heart of a good marriage. A man may propose to a woman via her family, with the first question posed to him being, "Do you work?" A valid question indeed. He may respond, "I am still looking", to which

[43] Al-Tirmidhī, *Jāmiʿ al-Tirmidhī*.

a blanket rejection is given. But a second man may propose who does work, yet does not pray. The family argues, however, "in shā' Allāh, he will start praying." Notice how in the affairs of dunyā, we find that our criteria is stiff and inflexible, but when it comes to dīn we are far more lax. Later on, we may be heartbroken to hear that he is abusing our daughter/sister, or that she is not giving her husband his rights. This can often be traced back to the maxim that "if an individual struggles to fulfil his obligations towards Allah ﷻ, then such an individual will most surely not fulfil his rights towards my daughter." For a Muslim woman, there is arguably no better protection in marriage than to be wed to a man who fears Allah ﷻ in his treatment of her.

Let us consider a reoccurring example of how problems develop later in life when this principle is not applied: it could be that a husband may decide to repent, having dropped the practice of a sinful habit and committing fully to the dīn, while his wife refuses to partake. The opposite may happen as well. This scenario only occurs when the two spouses were not on the same page to begin with. The very basis of such a marriage was not established upon the correct premise, the correct questions were not asked, the necessary investigations were not carried out, and the bigger picture was totally missed.

Ensure that your criteria is strong, that your vision is clear, and that you and your spouse share commitment to mutual goals.

The Prophet ﷺ declared:

الدُّنْيَا مَتَاعٌ وَخَيرُ مَتَاعِهَا المَرْأَةُ الصَّالِحَةُ

Life is an enjoyment and the greatest of its enjoyments is a righteous spouse.[44]

[44] Muslim, *Ṣaḥīḥ Muslim*.

At this juncture, it important to remember that righteousness is not limited to someone's outer appearance. For example, while a Muslim woman's veiling is undoubtedly part of her religious character, it is problematic and irresponsible to assume this as the be-all and end-all of religiosity. How "religious" is she, if, despite her pious attire, she is a backstabber, slanderer, habitual liar, foul-mouthed shapeshifter who changes her character according to her setting, or a schemer who causes endless problems between family members, friends, and community? Likewise, what can be said of a Muslim male who sports a well-groomed beard and long thobe, but is miserly with his family, manipulative in his dealings with others, and always searching for the faults of others?

The Prophet Muhammad ﷺ was asked:

يا رَسولَ اللهِ! إِنَّ فُلَانَةَ تَقُومُ اللَّيْلَ وَتَصُومُ النَّهارَ وَتَفْعَلُ
وَتَصَدَّقُ وَتُؤْذِي جِيرَانَهَا بِلِسَانِهَا

O Messenger of Allah, such and such lady prays at night, fasts during the day, carries out good deeds, gives charity but verbally harms her neighbours.

He ﷺ responded:

لَا خَيْرَ فِيهَا هِيَ مِنْ أَهْلِ النَّارِ

There is no good in her. She is among the people of the Hellfire.

He ﷺ was also asked:

وَفُلَانَةُ تُصَلِّي المَكْتُوبَةَ وَتَصَدَّقُ بِأَثْوَارٍ وَلَا تُؤْذِي أَحَدًا

Such and such lady who [only] prays her five daily prayers, gives out bits of curd as charity, but does not harm anyone.

He ﷺ responded, "She is of the people of Paradise."[45]

[45] Ibn Ḥanbal, *Musnad Aḥmad.*

Similarly, many assume that whoever wears a long beard, a short thobe, and perhaps a head covering of some sort has automatically passed the test of piety. Again, whilst no one can diminish from the religious nature of outward conformity to the Sunnah, it remains true that this person may fundamentally be anything but religious. He could still be perpetually aggressive, stingy, careless towards his familial duties, dealing with usury, alcohol, illicit relationships, and the like.

Bitter regret will inevitably catch up with those who, when choosing a spouse, forget that religion includes manners, considerate interactions with people, purity of heart, speech, behaviour and wealth. This is most certainly not confined to appearances. The Prophet ﷺ said:

أَكْمَلُ الْمُؤْمِنِينَ إِيمَانًا أَحْسَنُهُمْ خُلُقًا

The most perfect of believers with respect to *īmān* are those finest in their manners.[46]

What marrying a righteous person *does not* mean

It is critical for us to take a holistic approach whenever we offer an Islamic position on a topic, such that we attempt to analyse the entire collection of narrations on a matter to produce a well-rounded theory. Unfortunately, we often witness a binary approach to topics, bringing to light a handful of narrations (or sometimes even parts of narrations) whilst ignoring the broader corpus of Hadith and contextual considerations. This then produces a narrow and single dimensional outlook.

This is important to mention since in the topic of marriage, the criteria of righteousness in a spouse is often presented as

[46] Abū Dāwūd, *Sunan Abū Dāwūd*.

erasing every other criteria, as if the Shariah has emphasised only one matter. So, what does marrying a righteous person not entail?

The criterion of righteousness does not mean that the potential spouse is, for example, excused for being a self-imposed failure in life (e.g., not trying to earn a decent permissible income, sleeping half the day and waking up at midday, not wanting to graft for his family, etc.) but is somehow exempted from all this because of the apparent "righteousness" that the Hadith lists above all. Consider the other narrations that clearly identifies the value of a husband who endeavours to bring home an income. The Prophet ﷺ discouraged Fāṭimah bint Qays ﵂ from marrying Muʿāwiyah ﵁, saying:

أَمَّا مُعَاوِيَةُ فَصُعْلُوكٌ لاَ مالَ لَهُ

Muʿāwiyah is destitute with no money.[47]

Considerations like this demonstrate what it means to take a holistic approach in offering an Islamic perspective on a topic. Focusing on one narration alone and generalising its content is not only imbalanced, but it can be highly detrimental and even drive Muslims away from their faith. In this instance, focusing solely on religious commitment as the only criterion for marriage belies the numerous other qualities necessary for a healthy, flourishing marriage.

To further demonstrate, "righteousness" does not mean that a spouse is exempt from being loving, expressive and emotionally generous. The Prophet ﷺ who urged us "faẓfar bi dhāt al-dīn" (so seize the religiously committed one) also said:

خَيْرُ نِسَائِكُمُ الوَدُودُ الوَلُودُ، المُوَاتِيَةُ المُوَاسِيَةُ، إِذَا اتَّقَيْنَ اللهَ

[47] Ibn Ḥanbal, *Musnad Aḥmad.*

> The best of women are the loving, child-bearing, agreeable to their husbands, and comforting to them, on condition that they are God-fearing.[48]

Agreement and willingness within marriage manifests in the tone, manner, and lightness of everyday interactions with one another. Treating one another with affection can come from simple greetings or the relief of coming home to a warm welcome from your spouse. A person's commitment to their prescribed acts of worship is separate from this, and both need to be present for harmony in the relationship to be maintained.

Another misconception is that the criterion of righteousness means cultural compatibility is no longer a matter of concern. Kafā'ah (compatibility) is a matter that the religion gives weight to. In fact, the marital breakdown between the two noble Companions Zayd ibn Ḥārithah ﷺ and Zaynab bint Jaḥsh ﷺ was primarily due to an issue of compatibility.

Furthermore, the criterion of righteousness does not mean that families should delay marriage for a daughter who is ready, out of a belief that the ideal righteous suitor has not yet appeared. This rigid approach becomes particularly problematic when people are reaching the latter years of their youth. Concessions will need to be made – within reason, naturally. For example, a suitor arrives who does not sport a beard, or does not pray much in the mosque outside of the Friday prayers, or does not participate in Islamic activities outside of his basic worship, yet further delaying marriage may cause the sister at hand religious challenges. Should the potential match be given a blanket rejection based on the above considerations? A more nuanced approach is required.

[48] Al-Bayhaqī, *Al-Sunan al-Kubrā li al-Bayhaqī.*

Adopting a thorough vetting process

Once you have thought carefully about the qualities you wish to look for in a spouse, it is important to involve the trusted members of your family and community to establish the compatibility of a particular match. This is regardless of whether you have known of the person for a long time or were introduced to one another online. Doing "background checks" is a common process in which you enquire about the family, friends or even colleagues of a person you are considering, gauging their perspective on their character, Islamic commitment, background, and other priority areas. There are people who have known your potential spouse for decades and will be able to help you and your family by providing useful insights you could not have gleaned any other way, positive or negative. This will help you make a more confident, well-informed decision going forward. This also helps you deal with existing issues from the outset, avoiding complications later down the line when you are fully committed to one another.

Once background checks are performed, families should come together to get to know one another and discuss any issues relevant to the marriage. During this time, the girl's guardian (walī) and male family members often take the opportunity to speak to the potential husband to really gain a sense of who this person is, how serious his intentions are, and how compatible he will truly be with their daughter, sister, or relative.

This vetting process acts as an important safeguard for the woman that protects her interests – one that she should not belittle or even decide to forego altogether, in spite of the fact that it may seem inconvenient or excessively restrictive. A simple fact remains that men can read and scrutinise other men in a way women are rarely able to (and even less so when blinded by love). They will be able to discern practical issues that a woman may not even consider, yet are hugely important to the future of the marriage.

Another benefit of involving family at this stage is that once a woman's family is involved in the vetting process and have signed off on a choice of spouse, they are now ALL invested in making the marriage work and keeping the couple together. They will be on hand for mediation and advice as they will feel a partial sense of responsibility for the couple coming together in the first place. Research indicates supportive networks who are rooting for the couple are one of the best preventers of separation.

From the perspective of the man, a relationship he has had to work for and prove himself for is one he will value higher and be more mindful of preserving – the opposite of this is unfortunately also true. It is apparent that a man who has faced his future wife's family and their questions, knowing well what is expected of him, will generally be more careful of his overall conduct in the relationship. Understanding his responsibility to her family will raise the esteem he has for the marriage and therefore even temper his treatment of his spouse.

For the man who is being vetted by his potential wife's relatives, he should approach this process in a mature, understanding manner. He should know that, just as he is being put through the paces today, one day he too will – in shā' Allāh – scrutinise a potential match for his own future daughter. Your would-be wife is already somebody else's daughter.

In a climate where these safeguards are often belittled as infantilising women or infringing on their agency, it is important to embrace the necessary checks of the people who know you best. Marriage is a lifelong project and involves harmonising two families together (especially after you are blessed with children), so take advantage and draw strength from the support Allah ﷻ has blessed you with.

Putting this principle into practice

How can you attract this righteous individual into your life?

1. *Duʿā'*

There is one *duʿā'* that – if repeated with yaqīn (certainty) – you can be sure that Allah ﷻ will respond to and bless you with the finest of all spouses, and, if you are already married, you may be certain that Allah will beautify your current union and add to its richness and happiness.

This *duʿā'* can be found in Sūrah al-Furqān.

Allah ﷻ said:

وَالَّذِينَ يَقُولُونَ رَبَّنَا هَبْ لَنَا مِنْ أَزْوَاجِنَا وَذُرِّيَّاتِنَا قُرَّةَ أَعْيُنٍ وَاجْعَلْنَا لِلْمُتَّقِينَ إِمَامًا

And those who say, "Our Lord, grant us from among our spouses and offspring comfort to our eyes and make us an example for the righteous."[49]

2. *Istikharāh* (the prayer of consultation)

When the Prophet Muhammad ﷺ asked for the hand of Zaynab bint Jaḥsh رضي الله عنها in marriage, she said:

مَا أَنَا بِصَانِعَةٍ شَيْئًا حَتَّى أُؤَامِرَ رَبِّي

I will not decide on anything till I consult my Lord.[50]

Istikharāh is an indispensable gift to utilise over and over again in the process of finding a spouse. It is a short *duʿā'* that places your decision in the Hands of the One whose knowledge of

---

[49] *Al-Furqān*, 25:74.
[50] Muslim, *Ṣaḥīḥ Muslim.*

you and your needs is perfect and without oversight. Whichever stage of the marriage process you are in, use the istikharāh *du'ā'* to aid your decision making, and remain content that you are raising your hopes safely in the care of your Lord. Once you have decided and prayed istikharāh (as many times as you wish), you can enjoy the peace of mind that Allah ﷻ will bring forward only that which is in your benefit. Learn more about the etiquettes and conditions of istikharāh and use this *du'ā'* regularly for major and minor life decisions alike – those pertaining to marriage and those outside of it.

CHAPTER FOUR

On understanding differences

وَلَيْسَ الذَّكَرُ كَالْأُنْثَىٰ

And the male is not like the female.[51]

Of all the topics that fall under the banner of marriage, there are few as important to fully understand as the distinct complementary needs of men and women. We live in a time where the very idea of biology and gender is being eroded beyond recognition, such that the notion of psychological, emotional, and even practical differences between men and women are scorned as archaic, misogynistic, and repressive. Islam is a religion of parity and justice, however, and the unique creation of the male and female is something to be celebrated and honoured. The differences between the two sexes require understanding, empathy, and maturity so that – within a secure marriage – both husband and wife can thrive in harmony.

Before we delve deeper, let us begin by considering one of the most fundamental needs that human beings have: to be understood. Majority of the self-help market and media output is centred on the pain a person feels when they are not under-

[51] *Āl ʿImrān*, 3:36.

stood by others, whether this perception is real or perceived. To have a voice, be able to articulate your thoughts, and to have those feelings respected, validated, and honoured by the people you love is an empowering experience.

People have begun to realise that much of the pain in families is caused by a lack of understanding. If you look at the best-selling family books on the market today, you can get an idea of how significant this pain and this growing awareness is. Books such as Deborah Tannen's *You Just Don't Understand* and John Gray's *Men Are from Mars, Women Are from Venus* have not only become tremendously popular, but stood the test of time because they touch on this pain. Their enduring value illustrates how much people hunger to feel understood. The natural first step to being understood is to acknowledge that your spouse is different to you.

Islam acknowledges that there are clear differences between the genders, and reflects this in many of the rulings, whether in the departments of shahādah (testimony), inheritance, financial obligations, jihad, dress code, wearing jewellery, and even in acts of worship. Consider then, if the Shariah has acknowledged the differences between men and women and legislated accordingly, why does this appreciation not extend to our marital lives? One of the biggest mistakes we commit is when we judge one another according to a generic and idealised standard of behaviour without considering the particularities of each gender. In reality, it is an injustice to behave as though a husband and wife are on a level playing field when it comes to their personal, practical, emotional, and psychological needs.

Differences between the male and female

The argument of many contemporary feminists is that, despite the numerous biological, neurological, and physical differences between males and females, their roles and responsibilities should be as identical as possible. This is very counterintuitive. Even ancient models of justice, such as the Aristotelian principle, advocate to "treat like cases alike." In other words, matters that are similar ought to be treated in similar ways, and likewise different matters should be treated in different ways. Modern feminism simply does not accommodate for the real differences between men and women, and unquestionably this deliberate blind spot is a terminal failure that we do not need to accommodate. Rather, the burden of proof is not on us to demonstrate why we are right, but on them to show us why we are wrong. When they ask, "Why are the rulings different when it comes to inheritance, polygamy, and testimony, etc.?" the response is in fact to ask, "Why should they be the same?" The Qur'an says explicitly that the man is not like the woman, and accommodates for their differences appropriately.

These differences, it must be stressed, have no ethical value judgment attached, and do not indicate an increased worth of either the man or woman. You are both equal in the eyes of Allah ﷻ and both have identical access to the acceptance of Allah ﷻ and the bounties of the Hereafter. However, the identical value of men and women does not necessarily translate to having identical roles.

Sexual differences

A study by Roy Baumeister and Kathleen Vohs (2001) found that, "Across many different studies and measures, men have shown to have frequent and more intense sexual desires than women", a fact reflected in ten different facets that they cited.

No indications to the contrary were found in their study. In a different study, they posited that, "in sex, women are the suppliers and men constitute the demand." This is a description of general patterns, and it is important to remember that exceptions do of course exist in both men and women.

Hormonal differences

Women have 1/10th to 1/20th of testosterone in their bodies compared to men, which gives men physical advantages in strength, speed, muscle mass, and endurance, as was mentioned in an academic paper by David Handlesman.

Cognitive differences

In a study by Diane Halpern, she states that the differences in cognitive ability between the sexes is sizeable. A paper by Numrata Upadhayay concluded that although both males and females can compete equally in cognitive tasks, females outperformed males in attention-related tasks during the postovulatory phase of their menstrual cycles. This might be due to the effect of lowered testosterone.

Men and women are different in almost every area of life: they communicate, think, feel, perceive, react, respond, love, need and appreciate differently. The more we explore and understand these differences, the more we can begin to truly understand one another. We can then allow our masculine and feminine energies to act together, so they are complimentary rather than conflicting. If these fundamental differences have already created issues between husband and wife, then learning about them will mean that the barriers of resentment and misunderstandings will begin to melt away.

The primary motivators of men and women

Generally speaking, men are motivated and empowered when they feel needed, whilst women are motivated and empowered when they feel loved. This is because a man's sense of self is defined through his ability to achieve results. A man ultimately wishes to demonstrate his skills and competence, whereas a woman's sense of self is defined through her feelings and the quality of her relationships. For a man to feel redundant and not needed in his spouse's life can feel like a slow death.

Just appreciating this one difference can help dispel a huge variety of misunderstandings. It helps us understand why a man may feel sensitive when receiving unsolicited advice critical of him or his actions. To him, it is a presumption that he does not know what to do or that he cannot do it on his own. Similarly, we will understand why a woman may get annoyed when her husband offers solutions to her problems. He instantly puts on his "I can fix it" hat. That is his way of showing love, but in the world of womanhood, talking about problems is not always an invitation to offer a solution, but more, an invitation to have somebody listen, empathise, and offer comfort.

If you are a woman, I recommend that, for the next week, you practice restraining from giving any unsolicited advice or criticism on matters that can be delayed. The man in your life not only will appreciate it, but also will be more attentive and responsive to you. If you are a man, I suggest that, for the next week, you practice listening whenever your wife speaks, with the sole intention of respectfully understanding what she is going through. Practice biting your tongue whenever you get the urge to offer a solution or change how she is feeling. You will be surprised when you experience how much she then appreciates you.

Both men and women should stop offering the level of care which they would prefer for themselves, and instead start to learn the different ways their partners think, feel, and react.

The fears of men and women

The idea of receiving love can be very scary for some women. A woman may be afraid of needing "too much" and then being rejected, judged, or abandoned. Rejection, judgement, and abandonment are the most painful wounds a woman can receive, because deep inside her unconscious mind, she holds the fallacious belief that she is somehow unworthy of receiving more. These emotions are exacerbated if she had experienced neglect or letdowns in the past. A need for belonging puts her in a vulnerable position, and because she is afraid of not being supported she instinctively but unconsciously pushes away the support she needs.

Just as women can be afraid of receiving, some men can also be afraid of giving. To extend himself in giving – not just financially, but emotionally – means to risk rejection, correction, and disapproval. These consequences are most painful to a man, because deep inside his unconscious self, he then tells himself he is not good enough. This belief may have been formed and reinforced in childhood every time he thought he was expected to do better. Beneath his stoic exterior, he carries a huge fear of failure so he may not make extra efforts, and hence why he may come across as caring about only himself.

The love needs of men and women

"I love my wife" or "I love my husband" are statements readily announced by many a spouse, yet nevertheless, it is very common for one or both spouses to claim they do not feel loved by their partner. In many cases, this is because we have not understood what love means to our spouses nor appreciated the differing perceptions of love between men and women.

John Gray, author of *Men Are From Mars, Women Are From Venus,* has demonstrated how men and women prioritise their primary love needs differently.

Women often prioritise their prerequisities for love as:

1. Feeling cared about (implying uniqueness)
2. Feeling understood
3. Feeling respected
4. Feeling their partner's devotion
5. Feeling validated
6. Feeling reassured

Men often prioritise their needs for love as:

1. Feeling trusted (implying competence)
2. Feeling accepted
3. Feeling appreciated
4. Feeling admired
5. Feeling approved of
6. Feeling encouraged

Without understanding the needs and expectations of your partner as a man or a woman, you may try to give your spouse what you *yourself* would want, only for this to then backfire. For example, a husband whose wife is upset with him might back off to give her space, trusting her to work things out, just as he would do for another man and would want for himself. He takes her defeated cry of "leave me alone!" literally, only to regret it when he sees his wife is feeling unimportant, abandoned, and uncared for.

A wife, sensing her husband is upset, might push him to talk about his feelings (showing she cares about him, as she would with another woman and would want for herself). Her husband may feel pressured or smothered, in that scenario. Put yourself in the shoes of the other. So many problems are solved simply by virtue of understanding and acting according to the Qur'anic recognition that "the male is not like the female."

The existential needs of men and women

For men, respect regularly features at the top of the list of personal needs. A man not only wants to provide, but wants to be seen as the provider. Similarly, a woman wants security and in fact yearns to be *shown* security – that is financial, physical, religious, and emotional security. It is understandable why security may be at the top of her list of personal needs, just as it is understandable why a woman may, in the eyes of some men, "overreact" if a husband fails to pull his weight in searching for an adequate job, express lethargy when practicing Islam, or does not defend his wife in face of hostile parties (even and especially when hostility is expressed by either of their families); in her eyes, her security is being undermined, and this causes anxiety and concerns.

This is not about competition

A marriage is about *takāmul* – to complement one another. The Islamic model of marriage is one of complementarity over egality. Men and women were purposely designed to be different and mutually superior, exceeding one another in different ways and facets of life. There is profound wisdom in this, as it causes them to be better suited to work as a pair in pursuit of a common goal. Consider the following *āyah*:

وَلَا تَتَمَنَّوْا مَا فَضَّلَ ٱللَّهُ بِهِۦ بَعْضَكُمْ عَلَىٰ بَعْضٍ لِّلرِّجَالِ نَصِيبٌ مِّمَّا ٱكْتَسَبُوا وَلِلنِّسَآءِ نَصِيبٌ مِّمَّا ٱكْتَسَبْنَ وَسْـَٔلُوا ٱللَّهَ مِن فَضْلِهِۦٓ إِنَّ ٱللَّهَ كَانَ بِكُلِّ شَىْءٍ عَلِيمًا

And do not crave what Allah has given some of you over others. Men will be rewarded according to their deeds, and women will be equally rewarded according to theirs. Rather, ask Allah for His bounties. Surely Allah has perfect knowledge of all things.[52]

At peace with yourself is a result of being in line with your *fiṭrah*. Forgetting the centrality of *fiṭrah* means you will be engaged in a fight against your natural disposition, the outcome of which is misery, a sort of misery that befell the founding mothers of feminism with respect to their marital lives, despite many of them retracting their positions later on in life.

Betty Friedan, a leading feminist activist, who once described homes as a "comfortable concentration camp" later retracted this statement as being "rather extreme". After all their discussions and campaigning, she writes in her book *Second Stage* that young women were experiencing more signs of psychological stress and were more likely to feel on the edge of a nervous breakdown than young men.

Germaine Greer, one of the founding mothers of feminism, writes in her book *The Whole Woman* that "I still have pregnancy dreams, waiting with vast joy. Something that will never happen." Greer admits to continually mourning for her unborn babies, despite a career spent belittling the role of motherhood and ridiculing domesticity.

Simone de Beauvoir, who offered perhaps the most celebrated theories during the second wave feminism, ended up lamenting how ultimately useless her lifetime of pleasures and comfort would be, as she felt "cheated" believing she might leave behind something worthwhile after she left his world: Yet I loathe the

---

[52] *Al-Nisā'*, 4:32.

thought of annihilating myself quite as much now as I ever did. I think with sadness of all the books I've read, all the places I've seen, all the knowledge I've amassed, and that will be no more. All the music, all the paintings, all the culture, so many places: and suddenly nothing…If it had at least enriched the Earth; if it had given birth to…what? A hill? A rocket? But no. Nothing will have taken place. I can still see the hedge of hazel trees flurried by the wind and the promises with which I fed my beating heart while I stood gazing at the gold-mine at my feet: a whole life to live. The promises have all been kept. And yet, turning an incredulous gaze towards that young and credulous girl, I realise with stupor how much I was gypped.[53]

Blanchflower and Oswald conducted a study of 100,000 participants in the UK and US between 1970 and 1990s after the gender reform laws came into effect, and after the feminist movement had become entrenched, strengthened and more attractive to adopt. The outcome? Men were happier and women were sadder. Most damningly, it was found that legislative reforms had not been successful in improving the welfare of women in either country.

Conclusion

Relationship author Suzanne Venker writes: Anyone who enters marriage believing the institution is oppressive will never be successfully married. If you think sex roles are a result of a patriarchy designed to be unfair to women, rather than on what they're actually based on (the biological differences between the sexes), your relationship is doomed. A successful married relationship demands a deep understanding of biology and its role in the male-female dance. A strong marriage is in fact predicated on sexual differences or on how much couples let their differences shine.

---

[53] Simone de Beauvoir, *Forces of Circumstance*.

Men and women were created with differing anatomy for a reason – they are designed to work like a puzzle. If you want the pieces of a puzzle to work outside intimacy, then you need to know how and why the opposite gender thinks and behaves as they do. The mind of a man and the mind of a woman are just an different as their anatomy.

Polarity in a relationship is essential. It is the engine that makes the marriage move. Masculine energy conquers and reflects – it likes to do things. Feminine energy nurtures and verbalises – it likes to talk and to experience. That is why feminine energy is the receiver of masculine energy. It is why men typically make the first move in a relationship and the man normally proposes to the women rather than the other way round. On an archetypal level, the male acts and the female responds.

The fact that men are capable of nurturing and women are capable of conquering does not change the fact that this is typically not where each sex's natural energy flows. The more you understand and embrace this symbiosis, the more natural and conflict-free your relationship becomes. If you fight it, as the gender equality movement demands through their insistence that the sexes are interchangeable, the less successful you will be.

So many couples today, particularly younger people removed from traditional wisdom, pride themselves on having what they believe is an equal marriage by removing any semblance of gender roles. These folk are essentially in a fight with human nature – and we all know how that ends.

Men and women do not need to think and behave the same in order to be equal in value; they need only work together toward the same goal using their respective strengths, temperaments, and desires. Forcing men and women into the same box in order to score political points, although they naturally flow in different directions, will ultimately pull them apart. It may take ten or more years to happen, but rest assured, it inevitably will.[54]

Putting this principle into practice

You should actively read about the subject of differences in male and female psychology and relationship needs from reputable sources uninfluenced by gender abolitionists. Learn with the intention to be able to understand your spouse better so that you may respond to the needs they have, not the ones you have yourself or imagine your partner to have. It is helpful to learn about love languages as well as the personality type of your spouse. When it comes to relationship dynamics, some useful guides are *Men are from Mars and Women are from Venus* by John Gray as well as *The 7 Principles of Making Marriage Work* by John and Julia Gottman.

As a rule, set a target of communicating effectively with your spouse for a minimum of three hours a week for one month. During that time, if you are male, you should make a conscious effort to listen and empathise with your wife; if you are female, you should make a conscious effort to acknowledge your husband wherever possible and avoid potential criticism. Use this time to foster deeper, more sensitive, and meaningful conversations that may otherwise be buried under the responsibilities of everyday life, and make sure that all devices and distractions are turned off while doing so. Guard this time and use it as an opportunity to "check in" with one another in a way that is deeply fulfilling for both of your needs.

[54] Suzanne Venkler, "If you enter marriage thinking both sexes are the same, you'll never be successfully married." The Washington Examiner. November 25 2023. https://www.washingtonexaminer.com/opinion/if-you-enter-marriage-thinking-both-sexes-are-the-same-youll-never-be-successfully-married

CHAPTER FIVE

On inviting love and mercy

وَجَعَلَ بَيْنَكُم مَّوَدَّةً وَرَحْمَةً

And He has placed between you affection and mercy.[55]

Love and mercy are two of the most powerful forces that can exist between people in a committed marital bond, and provide the most secure protection against life's inevitable adversities. In the realm of human connection, a marital relationship of love defies comparison to all else. This is a love woven with the threads of passion, trust, and vulnerability. It allows us to bare our true selves without fear of judgment or rejection. It allows us to navigate the unpredictable paths of life hand in hand, finding comfort and strength in the embrace of eternal partnership.

Love and mercy within marriage transcend the boundaries of time, echoing throughout the ages as a testament to the power of Allah ﷻ, who has harnessed this miraculous human connection. Indeed, people of every culture and background will all testify to how true marital love can foster one of the greatest joys there is in life. I will share with you a few such examples from the Islamic tradition.

[55] *Al-Rūm*, 30:21.

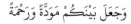

Testimonies of Love

Our Mother ʿĀ'ishah ﵂ said:

I was never more jealous of any of the wives of the Prophet as I was of Khadījah ﵂, even though I had never seen her.[56] This was because of how much the Prophet ﷺ used to make mention of her. He would at times slaughter a sheep, cut it to pieces and distribute its meat to the friends of Khadījah. At times, I would say to him, "

It is as if there is no woman on Earth but Khadījah!", to which he would respond:

إِنَّهَا كَانَتْ وكَانَتْ وكَانَ لِي منها ولَدٌ

She was this and she was that, and I have children from her.[57]

She ﵂ also said, "On one occasion, I angered him, having said 'Khadījah!' (i.e., you always talk about her!), to which he responded,

إِنِّي قد رُزِقْتُ حُبَّهَا

I have been blessed with her love.[58]

In fact, in a touching incident that occurred after the death of the Prophet ﷺ, Hālah ﵂ bint Khuwaylid – Khadījah's sister – sought permission to enter upon the Prophet ﷺ. Upon hearing her voice, he ﷺ was reminded of Khadījah's manner of seeking permission and was deeply moved by it, saying with affection:

[56] Khadījah ﵂ had passed away before ʿĀ'ishah ﵂ had become the Prophet's wife.

[57] Al-Bukhārī, *Ṣaḥīḥ al-Bukhārī.*

[58] Muslim, *Ṣaḥīḥ Muslim.*

اللَّهُمَّ هَالَةُ بِنْتُ خُوَيْلِدٍ

O Allah it is Hālah, daughter of Khuwaylid!

On one occasion, our Mother ʿĀ'ishah's jealousy drove her to say:

ما أكثرَ ما تذكُرُها حَمراءَ الشِّدْقِ قد أبدَلَكَ اللهُ عزَّ وجلَّ بها خيرًا منها

How often will you remember an old woman [with a toothless mouth] of red gums in whose place Allah has given you somebody better than her!

Showing respect to both of his wives, the Prophet ﷺ responded:

ما أبدَلَني اللهُ عزَّ وجلَّ خيرًا منها، قد آمَنَتْ بي إذ كفَرَ بي الناسُ
وصدَّقَتْني إذ كذَّبَني الناسُ وواسَتْني بمالِها إذ حرَمَني الناسُ ورزَقَني اللهُ
عزَّ وجلَّ ولَدَها إذ حرَمَني أولادَ النِّساءِ

No, Allah has not substituted me with someone better than her. She had faith in me when others disbelieved; she believed me when others belied me; she comforted me with her wealth when others deprived me; and Allah blessed me with children through her and withheld them from other women.[59]

A deep level of enduring love was something that featured in the lives and marriages of other Companions ﷺ as well.

Six months after the passing of the Prophet Muhammad ﷺ, his daughter Fāṭimah ﷺ left this world too. Her husband, ʿAlī ibn Abī Ṭālib ﷺ, stood at her graveside and tearfully uttered the following couplets of poetry:

مالِي وَقَفتُ عَلى القُبورِ مُسَلِّماً * قَبرَ الحَبيبِ فَلَم يَرُدَّ جَوابي

"What is wrong with me, standing at the graveside saying *salām* to the one who has passed? The grave of my beloved, but she does not respond to my greeting.

[59] Ibn Ḥanbal, *Musnad Aḥmad.*

أَحَبيبُ مالَكَ لا تَرُدُّ جَوابَنا * أَنَسيتَ بَعدي خِلَّةَ الأَحبابِ

My beloved, why do you not respond to my *salām*? Have you forgotten all the intimate moments that were shared between us?

قالَ الحَبيبُ وَكَيفَ لي بِجَوابِكُم * وَأَنا رَهينُ جَنادِلٍ وَتُرابِ

But the beloved responded, "How can I respond to you, whilst I am now the captive of stones and dirt?

أَكَلَ التُرابُ مَحاسِني فَنَسيتُكُم * وَحُجِبتُ عَن أَهلي وَعَن أَترابي

The dirt has consumed my beauty and that is why I have moved on. And I have been veiled from my family and my loved ones.

فَعَلَيكُمُ مِنّي السَلامَ تَقَطَّعَت * مِنّي وَمِنكُم خِلَّةَ الأَحبابِ

So my *salām* back to you and to them – those intimate moments have now passed!"

It is often said that grief is the price we pay for love. We observe the intensity of that love present in the words of female Companions like Umm Salamah, who could not comprehend a greater goodness than the love she shared with her husband:

When Abū Salamah passed away, his widow – Umm Salamah – said, "I heard the Prophet say:

ما مِن مُسْلِمٍ تُصِيبُهُ مُصِيبَةٌ فيقولُ ما أَمَرَهُ اللَّهُ إِنَّا لِلَّهِ وَإِنَّا إِلَيْهِ رَاجِعُونَ
اللَّهُمَّ أْجُرْنِي في مُصِيبَتِي وأَخْلِفْ لي خَيْرًا مِنْها، إلَّا أخْلَفَ اللَّهُ له خَيْرًا مِنْها

Any Muslim who is befallen with a calamity but says, "*Innā li Allāh, wa innā ilayhi rājiʿūn* (to Allah we belong, and to Him we shall return), O Allah reward me for my calamity and grant me in its place that which is better", Allah will grant him what is better.

Umm Salamah commented on this Hadith, adding "I said to myself, which Muslim could be better than Abū Salamah? His was the first household to migrate to the Prophet Muhammad. Nevertheless, I uttered those words and Allah did indeed grant me what is better; the Prophet Muhammad ﷺ (whom she married)."[60]

What is obvious to note from her words above is the sheer love, adoration, and high regard that Umm Salamah ﵂ had for her husband, all captured in her simple question, "Which Muslim could be better than Abū Salamah?"

Love can drive humans to unimaginable lengths, allowing them to defy all rationality, limitations, and boundaries. When it comes to the power of marital love, let us turn our attention to what Umm Ḥākim ﵂ was willing to do for the protection and security of her husband, who was not only a polytheist at the time, but also one of the fiercest enemies of the Prophet ﷺ.

ʿIkrimah ibn Abī Jahl ﵁ fought the Muslims fiercely till the very last hour at the Conquest of Makkah. The Prophet ﷺ pardoned the entire city with the exception of a few war criminals. ʿIkrimah ﵁ was in fact one of those exceptions. ʿIkrimah ﵁ fled Makkah and headed towards the direction of Yemen, and to reach his destination, opted to board a boat. He was startled, however, to see his wife Umm Ḥakīm ﵂, who had caught up with him. After embracing Islam, she had approached the Prophet ﷺ, asking him to pardon her husband ʿIkrimah ﵁. The Prophet ﷺ agreed, but she requested this pardon in writing, which was granted to her.

She had arrived at the coast moments before her husband's voyage, giving him the good news of his safety, saying, "O son of ʿAmr! I have a pledge of peace from the Prophet ﷺ. So, if you embrace Islam and accept this pledge, then I will remain your wife. Otherwise, all connections between us will be severed."

However, ever proud and hard-hearted, he did not even turn his face to look at her and set sail. During the journey, the waves

[60] Muslim, *Ṣaḥīḥ Muslim*.

grew turbulent, causing ʿIkrimah ﵁ to mutter polytheistic prayers to his idols. The boat's captain said to him:

أَخْلِصْ فَإِنَّهُ لَنْ يُنْجِيكَ إِلَّا الإِخْلَاصَ

Be sincere (i.e., devote your prayers to the One God), for nothing will save you but sincerity.

Upon hearing that, it was as if the veils of arrogance were at once lifted from his sight. There, amid the turmoil of stormy seas, ʿIkrimah ﵁ was reminded of a reality that he knew too well but had been too haughty to surrender to – that the Prophet Muhammad ﷺ was indeed a Messenger of God.

ʿIkrimah ﵁ said, "It seems that I am fleeing from the truth." He was finally ready to put an end to his years of internal warfare and to make peace with himself. So, at once, he would travel back to Mecca, making his way to the Prophet ﷺ, where he would embrace Islam.

What was it that drove Umm Ḥakīm ﵂ to do what she did? Her husband was not a Muslim and not even showing the slightest interest in the truth, yet she was a woman who loved – and therefore wanted goodness – for her husband. Umm Ḥakīm ﵂ went to the extent of obtaining a written agreement from the Prophet ﷺ to save her husband's life, and then ran desperately to the coast to appeal to her husband. All of this meant she eventually became the cause of his accepting Islam and one day becoming one of the finest and noblest martyrs of the religion. What was the catalyst for all this? Nothing but her pure love and mercy for him.

Further examples show us how the depth of a person's love can manifest most strongly when they are forced to depart from their beloved. To this end, Ibn Zurayq al-Baghdādī, an Iraqi poet who lived nearly a millennium ago, described the heart wrenching moments when he bade his wife farewell before embarking on a business trip, for the voyage would not only cost him years of forced separation, but would ultimately end in his death far from home.

He said:

أَسْتَوْدِعُ اللهَ فِي بَغْدَادَ لِي قَمَرًا * بِالكَرْخِ مِنْ فَلَكِ الأَزْرَارِ مَطْلَعُهُ

I bid farewell to a moon in Baghdad, that rises over the skies above Karkh.

وَدَّعتُهُ وَبِوُدِّي لَوْ يُوَدِّعُنِي * صَفْوَ الحَياةِ وَأَنِّي لَا أُوَدِّعُهُ

I bid her farewell whilst wishing that I was bidding farewell to the serenity of life instead.

وَكَمْ تَشَفَّعَ بِي أَلَا أُفَارِقُهُ * وَلِلْضَرُورَاتِ حَالٌ لَا تُشفِّعهُ

How frequently did she plead that I not leave, but necessity leaves one without options!

وَكَم تَشبَّثَ بِي يَومَ الرَّحِيلِ ضُحًى * وَأَدْمُعِي مُستَهِلّاتٌ وَأَدمُعُهُ

How intensely she held onto me on the noon of my departure, whilst tears flowed from my eyes and hers!

وَمَنْ يُصَدِّعُ قَلْبِي ذِكْرَهُ وَإِذَا * جَرَى عَلَى قَلْبِهِ ذِكْرِي يُصَدِّعُهُ

She is the one who causes my heart to ache in her remembrance, and I am the one who causes her heart to ache at my remembrance.

These feelings of deep love and attachment regularly characterise our tradition, especially for those who were forced to depart from their beloved spouses out of necessity, not choice. When Imam Ibn Ḥajar ﵁ travelled in pursuit of sacred knowledge, he wrote the following couplets of poetry, depicting his longing for his wife, Laylā al-Ḥalabiyyah ﵂:

رَحَلْتُ وَخَلَّفْتُ الحَبِيبَ بِدَارِهِ * بِرَغْمِي وَلَمْ أَجْنَحْ إِلَى غَيْرِهِ مَيْلَا

أُشَاغِلُ نَفْسِي بِالحَدِيثِ تَعَلُّلاً * نَهَارِي وَفِي لَيْلِي أَحِنُّ إِلَى لَيْلَى

I have departed, leaving behind the beloved against my will, and never did my heart incline to other than her.

I busy myself throughout the day with the study of Hadith to distract it, but when the night arrives, my heart yearns for Laylā.[61]

When it comes to the ultimate separation of death, the longing for closeness to the beloved burned in the hearts of those such as the poet Yaḥyā al-Hindī al-Andalūsī ﵀, who authored a famous couplet of poetry on the subject shortly before he passed away:

إِذَا مِتُّ فَادْفِنِّي حِذَاءَ خَلِيلَتِي * يُخَالِطُ عَظْمِي فِي التُّرَابِ عِظَامَهَا

وَرَتِّبْ ضَرِيحِي كَيْفَمَا شَاءَهُ الهَوَى * تَكُونُ أَمَامِي أَوْ أَكُونُ أَمَامَهَا

If I die, bury me besides my soulmate, so that my bones from beneath the soil can mix with hers.

Arrange my resting place according to my wishes, regardless of whether she is ahead of me, or I am ahead of her.[62]

Such examples of marital love and mercy are endless and span across all civilisations and eras of human history. Nevertheless, even relationships like these are not without their trials, since this world is oftentimes a turbulent sea where storms forever brew and waves crash hard. Yet, amidst this chaos, a loving marriage can stand as an unwavering beacon, a lighthouse guiding travellers through the dark nights. This is because a Muslim marriage is fortified not only with love alone. When such heartfelt sentiments are weathered away by the storms of life, the ensuing conflicts are quelled and wounds are healed through the quality of mercy, for Allah ﷻ said, "And He has placed between you affection and mercy."

[61] Al-Sakhāwī, *al-Ḍaw' al-Lāmiʿ.*

[62] Lisān al-Dīn ibn al-Khaṭīb, *al-Iḥāṭah fī Akhbār Gharnāṭah.*

For this reason, Imam Ibn Kathīr h wrote in his Qur'anic commentary:

فَإِنَّ الرَّجُلَ يُمْسِكُ الْمَرْأَةَ إِمَّا لِمَحَبَّتِهِ لَهَا أَوْ لِرَحْمَةٍ بِهَا بِأَنْ يَكُونَ لَهَا مِنْهُ وَلَدٌ أَوْ مُحْتَاجَةٌ إِلَيْهِ فِي الْإِنْفَاقِ أَوْ لِلْأُلْفَةِ بَيْنَهُمَا وَغَيْرِ ذَلِكَ

It could be that a man remains with his wife due to the love which he has for her, or for his sense of mercy towards her due to the children he has from her, or for the fact that she may be financially dependent on him, or due to their closeness, or other reasons.[63]

In many films and popular media of our times, relationships are often portrayed as all-or-nothing situations, such that if one person falls out of love with their partner, the relationship is automatically doomed and needs to end. However, in reality, relationships are much more complex and nuanced than this. Love is just one aspect of a relationship, and its presence and intensity can fluctuate from time to time. Relationships are built on a variety of factors, including shared values, mutual respect, communication, trust, companionship, and mercy. While love is important, it is not the sole determinant of a successful relationship.

Accordingly, when a man came to ʿUmar ﵁ wanting to divorce his wife, arguing that he "does not love her anymore", ʿUmar ﵁ responded:

وَيْحَكَ! أَوَكُلُّ الْبُيُوتِ تُبْنَى عَلَى الْحُبِّ، فَأَيْنَ الرِّعَايَةُ؟ وَأَيْنَ التَّذَمُّمُ؟

Woe to you! Is every household built upon love?! What happened to care and the shame brought on from being the cause of a family breakup?

While divorce is a valid option in cases of irreconcilable differences or when a relationship becomes unhealthy or abusive,

[63] Ibn Kathīr, *Tafsīr Ibn Kathīr*.

it is not advisable to resort to divorce as a knee-jerk reaction to temporary perceptions that love is fading away. The long journey of marriage will include questionable times, yet these are storms to be weathered, and should not be a cause for despair.

Similarly, when a man came to ʿUmar ﷺ complaining to him that his wife told him that she hates him, he summoned his wife and asked her regarding this. She responded, "Yes, because he asked me in Allah's name if I hate him, and so I did not want to lie." ʿUmar ﷺ responded,

بَلَى فَلْتَكْذِبْ إِحْدَاكُنَّ وَلْتُجْمِلْ فَلَيْسَ كُلُّ الْبُيُوتِ تُبْنَى عَلَى الْحُبِّ
وَلَكِنْ مُعَاشَرَةٌ عَلَى الْأَحْسَابِ وَالْإِسْلَامِ

> No, she should lie in this circumstance and should speak generally, for not all households are built upon love, but rather, at times living well together is built upon the duty of lineage and Islam.[64]

As the years roll on and the fervour of youth fades, the nature of your relationship will evolve. Responsibilities and various factors such as stress, life changes, personal challenges, or financial difficulties may wear a partnership down. The power of true love and mercy is that it will endure and manifest even in the most difficult and challenging chapters of life. The youthful passion you once had will mature into a love that has been tempered by the hands of time. If both individuals are committed to the relationship and are willing to work on it, they will more often than not overcome these difficulties and rebuild their connection with each other. It is possible for partners to rekindle their love or find new ways to appreciate each other, even when the initial romantic spark has inevitably faded. It is at those times particularly that mercy comes to play its role.

[64] Al-Ṭabarī, *Tahdhīb al-Āthār.*

If a couple were to contemplate divorce and remarriage every time their feelings of love wane, then everyone would be constantly changing partners, chasing a high that is never meant to last in the first place. A secure marriage requires nurture, effort, and understanding, and you cannot rely on fleeting emotions for this.

Real, lasting love becomes stronger and meaningful as the marriage progresses. It is an ongoing journey of discovery and deepening connection. While the early stages of a relationship may be filled with excitement, chemistry, and the thrill of discovering each other, it is through the passage of time and shared experiences that love strengthens and matures. As partners spend more time together, they become intimately acquainted with each other's quirks, idiosyncrasies, and vulnerabilities. They learn to accept and appreciate each other for who they truly are, embracing both the strengths and imperfections of the one they love most.

In short, even if feelings of love or being loved waver during a marriage, the presence of mercy can act as a healing force, allowing spouses to bridge any emotional gap between them and restore their connection in a way that is often even stronger than before.

Putting this principle into practice

It is no exaggeration to say that, unfortunately, the world today is antagonistic to the very concept of marriage itself, doing everything it can to prevent marriages from thriving and remaining healthy in the long haul. In the reality of everyday life, there is a seemingly endless list of concerns that compete to snatch away your spouse's attention until the state of your marriage falls to the bottom of an interminably long priority list. As the two people in the marriage, it is your mutual responsibility to do the work of keeping the connection between yourselves alive. Just as homes require physical maintenance, the love within them needs regular check-ins, refreshes, and at times, perhaps even wholesale refurbishments.

This is a true principle for all relationships: you gain according to the effort you put into it. View your marriage as a top priority and put aside time, energy (and if necessary, finances) to improve, refine, and polish the state of it. The consequence of not doing so are often terminal in a relationship – when other activities (or even people) fill the space meant for husband and wife, two people will become strangers under the same roof.

In physics, this principle is mirrored when we consider the reality of "entropy". This means that anything left to itself will eventually disintegrate until it reaches its most elemental form. Do not allow your marriage to degenerate to simply a living arrangement ridden with joyless responsibilities. Anything that is not consciously tended to and renewed will break down, become disordered, and deteriorate. Your marriage is far too precious to reach this state, and so here are a few suggestions to keep your marriage strong and healthy:

1. Love for Allah's sake

True love is to love someone so much that you want your love for them to last beyond this lifetime and into the Hereafter, where you can live in eternal happiness with them enjoying Allah's pleasure together. It means you love someone purely because of how much they remind you of Allah ﷻ and help you get closer to Him. Hold it right there. I know what you just thought – "*But my wife/husband does not remind me of Allah at all.*"

A lot of people who marry each other even for primarily religious reasons end up disappointed after marriage when they suddenly find their spouse not praying all the Sunnah prayers (like they thought they would), reading the Qur'an every day, doing the morning and evening *adhkār*, fasting Mondays and Thursdays, being excited about attending *ḥalaqahs*, praying *tahajjud*, or making efforts for the Ummah – *like they thought they would.* When we restrict our spirituality to acts of physical or outward worship, we can become blinded from seeing how much our spouse contributes to our lives. Do not box up someone's *īmān* into overly restrictive notions of goodness.

Your spouse has loved you for Allah's sake every time they have reminded you to call your parents, stopped you from backbiting others, helped you to preserve your chastity, said something as simple as "*yarḥamuk Allāh*" (may Allah have mercy upon you) after you sneeze, encouraged you to wake up to pray, and watched or attended Islamic lectures with you.

In all of these common occurrences, and in so many other moments that go unnoticed, committed Muslim spouses consistently help each other get closer to Allah ﷻ. Appreciate this and do not allow the gems at your feet to go unnoticed while you look for jewels on the horizon elsewhere.

2. The giving of gifts

The act of gift-giving has long been a phenomenon studied by those interested in human behaviour, especially as it relates to creating and strengthening bonds between people. For this reason, it is extensively studied by psychologists, anthropologists, sociologists, economists and marketers. Overall, it has been found that giving gifts is a surprisingly complex and important part of human interaction that serves to define relationships and strengthen bonds with family and friends.

The Prophet ﷺ said:

تَهَادُوا تَحَابُّوا

Give gifts to one another and you will
love one another.[65]

For many people, the practice of gift-giving is limited to the days when they were courting their spouse in a bid to make the best impression. In those pre-marital days, you would not show up without designer bags, big bouquets of flowers and elaborate sweet treats in your hand to show your potential spouse how important they were to you. Why is it, now that you are married, there is suddenly no need for gifts anymore, such that only ever coming home with grocery bags is sufficient?

Generous gift-giving is not just an investment in your relationship, but an investment into your own wellbeing too. The act of gift giving is one that gives right back! Indeed, psychologists say it is often the giver, rather than the recipient, who reaps the biggest psychological gains from a gift, witnessing the joy they have brought to the other person. Revive this Sunnah and watch your relationship flourish as a result!

3. Dedicate uninterrupted time to attentive talk

Traditional Muslim scholars have noted and commented on the attentive listening skills of the Prophet Muhammad ﷺ with his wife ʿĀ'ishah ؓ, as was clearly demonstrated in the famous Hadith of Umm Zarʿ. On one evening when the Prophet ﷺ was with ʿĀ'ishah ؓ, she told him the story of eleven women who gathered and promised each other that they would speak about their husbands without concealing any news. In a display of her phenomenal memory, ʿĀ'ishah ؓ narrated word for word what each of the eleven women had said about their

[65] Al-Bukhārī, *Ṣaḥīḥ al-Bukhārī.*

husbands, some of whom spoke highly of their spouses whilst others spoke critically.

The most striking of the descriptions, however, was that of the eleventh woman, Umm Zarʿ who lavishly praised her husband, Abū Zarʿ, along with every matter connected to him. His only flaw was that Abū Zarʿ once saw another woman whom he was attracted to, and so he divorced Umm Zarʿ and married the other.

Umm Zarʿ remarried a brave and noble man who was a good husband to her and provided abundantly for both her and her relatives, yet none of this would match the memory of her former husband, and so she said, "Yet, all those things which my second husband gave me could not fill the smallest utensil of Abū Zarʿ."

Upon hearing this extensive narration, the Prophet ﷺ said to ʿĀ'ishah رضي الله عنها:

كُنْتُ لَكِ كَأَبِي زَرْعٍ لِأُمِّ زَرْعٍ، إِلَّا أَنَّ أَبَا زَرْعٍ طَلَّقَ وَأَنَا لَا أُطَلِّقُ

I have been to you as Abū Zarʿ was to Umm Zarʿ,[66] except that Abu Zarʿ divorced his wife, and I will not divorce you.[67]

The response of the Prophet ﷺ demonstrates how, not only did he listen attentively to every aspect of his wife's story, but he processed it entirely and used it as an opportunity to reaffirm his love and commitment to her. For this reason, Imam al-Bukhārī رحمه الله titled the chapter of this Hadith:

بَابُ حُسْنِ الْمُعَاشَرَةِ مَعَ الأَهْلِ

Chapter: Treating family in a polite and kind manner

[66] Al-Bukhārī, *Ṣaḥīḥ al-Bukhārī;* Muslim, *Ṣaḥīḥ Muslim.*
[67] Al-Ṭabarānī, *Muʿjam al-Kabīr li al-Ṭabarānī.*

Make an intention to decompress in one another's company each evening. It is not difficult to schedule in at least half an hour of undivided attention and attentiveness to your spouse. Think long term. Before you know it, your bosses and jobs will have changed, you will be retiring and replaced, and the kids you have raised would have married and moved out. The only person you will be left with is that spouse you spent a lifetime putting in second place. This same spouse will have become so used to being neglected over the past decades of your marriage that they have learnt to live independently of you and will be utterly indifferent to your presence. These are the years to invest in your marital bond, so you will have that warm companion you will desperately need and appreciate so much in your old age.

Emotional abandonment is often cited as one of the key reasons for women filing for divorce. Statistics also show women are the key consumers of books on marriage, and initiate counselling and therapy much more frequently than men. Yet, women also file for divorce twice as often as men. What is happening here?

Emotional abuse and spousal neglect are often grouped together as common reasons why women initiate divorce, though these are often less understood or accepted as valid grievances. Likewise, it is often said that "women leave a marriage years before they leave a marriage." What this means in practical terms is that a woman may make efforts (issuing "bids for attention") to initiate connection, but if these are repeatedly ignored, mocked, scorned or stone-walled by their husbands, then they can mentally check out of the relationship and decide that their marriages are not spaces in which they can have their needs met.

Building an emotional connection should never be belittled or waved away as unnecessary; this is the cornerstone of a strong marriage. Begin with conversations where you listen with the intention to understand your spouse and truly make them feel heard and respected. Schedule in these moments of connection if your lifestyles are hectic, and preserve them at all costs. The foundation for love is understanding and connection.

Though people may immediately protest, "We do not have the time!", if they were honest to themselves, what they would say instead is "It is not important enough", hence revealing the truth of what (or who) is significant in our lives. The place to start is not with the assumption that work is non-negotiable; it is that my family and marriage are non-negotiable. That one shift of mindset opens the door to reinvigorating your marriage.

To cultivate attentive listening, it is important to be present in the moment, maintain eye contact, and minimise distractions. Show interest through verbal and non-verbal cues, such as nodding, summarizing what you heard, and asking clarifying questions. Most importantly, practice empathy and genuine curiosity to truly understand your spouse's perspective.

4. Be the comfort of each other's eyes

You are the only man/woman whom your spouse is allowed to look at from head to toe, so please do not be an eyesore. Make this your mantra. Remind yourself of this when you feel it is not "worth the effort" to take care of your hair, figure, scent, and clothing.

Allah ﷻ said:

وَالَّذِينَ يَقُولُونَ رَبَّنَا هَبْ لَنَا مِنْ أَزْوَاجِنَا وَذُرِّيَّاتِنَا قُرَّةَ أَعْيُنٍ وَجْعَلْنَا لِلْمُتَّقِينَ إِمَامًا

And those who say, "Our Lord, grant us from among our wives and offspring comfort to our eyes and make us an example for the righteous.[68]

---

[68] *Al-Furqān*, 25:74.

These daily efforts do not have to be elaborate either. It does not take long to have a quick shower, put on some nice clothes, apply perfume, comb your hair, and put on a dash of make-up. These extra moments of grooming go a long way in a relationship, no matter how many years pass. In a sea of impermissible sights that your spouse has protected themselves from, make the permissible sight of you something worth looking forward to. Incorporate this focus on showing your spouse the best of you into a fixed part of your routine, ideally just before your spouse gets home or before you sit down to relax together.

5. Social media

When you truly love and value your spouse, you will stop seeking attention from others. Those who find joy in the opinions of others will never be satisfied with the attention, validation, and admiration they get, as their appetite for it only grows.

You can't love and be attentive to your spouse when you're preoccupied with worrying about what others think of you and how you might next impress them. Whether it is posting pictures on social media, buying homes to compete with others, or going on lavish holidays – ask yourself what purpose you are truly doing all this for? What is driving the need within you, and is it coming at the cost of your spouse's needs? Scale back social media use to the absolute bare minimum.

6. Don't show the world

Privacy is a concept all but abandoned in today's world. Nothing is sacred anymore; in fact, it is splattered all over the internet for the world to see. Everywhere we go, everything we do – all of it is made public for the eye of those who know you or do not, and those who wish you well or do not. Instead of enjoying the moment, we get lost in cyberspace, trying to figure out the best status update, witty caption, or the perfect filter. Your private life contains the most important things of this world in it: your spouse, children, and family. Do not diminish its value by presenting it all on the public stage for the eyes of others to devour.

The Prophet Muhammad ﷺ said:

إِذَا رَأَى أَحَدُكُمْ مَا يُعْجِبُهُ فِي نَفْسِهِ أَوْ مَالِهِ فَلْيُبَرِّكْ عَلَيْهِ فَإِنَّ العَيْنَ حَقٌّ

If one of you sees something of himself, or one's wealth, or of his brother's that catches his eye, let him make *du'ā'* that Allah blesses it, for the evil eye is real.[69]

The Prophet Muhammad ﷺ also said:

إِنَّ العَيْنَ لَتُدْخِلُ الرَّجُلَ القَبْرَ وَالجَمَلَ القِدْرَ

The evil eye drives man to his grave and the camel to the pot.[70]

Muslim couples today are serving their marriages on exquisitely decorated social media platters for the evil eye to feast upon – not just the ceremony, but every single verbal and non-verbal marital exchange, meal, meeting, moment, mood and micro-second between husband and wife. Not only is it unnecessary, and highly insensitive to people who are struggling to get married or with bad marriages, but very damaging to your own relationship.

Though believers are never meant to be paranoid, protecting your relationship from the evil eye is the first way to guard against harm. Be diligent in reading your morning and evening adhkār, brush up on the *du'ā'* prescribed for protection against the evil eye, and constantly thank Allah ﷻ for your marriage and your spouse. This will strengthen this protection immensely, while allowing you to enjoy your life with peace of mind and heart.

---

[69] Ibn Ḥanbal, *Musnad Aḥmad*.

[70] Al-Bukhārī, *Ṣaḥīḥ al-Bukhārī;* Muslim, *Ṣaḥīḥ Muslim*.

Look after what is precious and protect the blessings gifted to you by your Lord.

CHAPTER SIX

On mutual consultation

فَإِنْ أَرَادَا فِصَالًا عَن تَرَاضٍ مِّنْهُمَا وَتَشَاوُرٍ فَلَا جُنَاحَ عَلَيْهِمَا

And if they both desire weaning through mutual agreement from both of them and consultation, there is no blame upon either of them.[71]

You may wonder how an *āyah* about breastfeeding is relevant to maintaining a strong marriage. For context, this verse gives us an insight into how parents should make decisions around weaning their child. After speaking of several rulings regarding breastfeeding, Allah ﷻ pre-empts the question of whether parents can decide to wean children earlier than this prescribed time. The answer? They are permitted to do that, as long as there is "mutual consent" and "consultation" involved.

In the manner that Allah ﷻ instructs two spouses to behave when deciding on the matter of breastfeeding a baby, then it is clear that we must implcment the same conduct throughout our entire married lives – whether for minor or major decisions.

How often do a husband and wife consult one another? Some men may feel that by consulting their wife, their leadership is called into question. Similarly, a wife may feel that needing to consult with her husband is a sign of his "toxic masculinity",

[71] *Al-Baqarah*, 2:233.

"male chauvinism", or "controlling behaviour". Both of these attitudes have no basis in the Sunnah. Our Prophet ﷺ, the most complete and perfect of all mankind, did not fear this. If anyone risked being undermined by asking for a second opinion, it would have been the Prophet ﷺ, since he was one of the most observed men in the world, watched by friend and foe alike.

When the very first verses of revelation came to the Prophet ﷺ, he was overcome with a mixture of worry, anxiety, and unrest over what had just occurred. What had happened? What had he heard? Was he losing his mind? In a state of intense fear, he returned to his wife – and confidante – Khadījah bint Khuwaylid رضي الله عنها and told her everything. After listening attentively, she was asked for her thoughts on the incident, and the beautiful exchange in the following conversation unfolded:

"O Khadījah!", cried out the Prophet ﷺ, "What is wrong with me? I was afraid that something bad might happen to me." Khadījah رضي الله عنها immediately moved to give a full, swift, and reassuring affirmation to her husband in his most pressing time of need, saying:

كَلَّا وَاللَّهِ مَا يُخْزِيكَ اللَّهُ أَبَدًا، إِنَّكَ لَتَصِلُ الرَّحِمَ وَتَحْمِلُ الكَلَّ وَتَكْسِبُ
المَعْدُومَ وَتَقْرِي الضَّيْفَ وَتُعِينُ عَلَى نَوَائِبِ الحَقِّ

Never! By Allah, Allah will never disgrace you! For you keep good relations with your family, help the poor and the destitute, serve your guests generously and assist in noble causes.[72]

These words were the balm that soothed the panicked heart and racing thoughts of the Messenger of Allah ﷺ who was not too shy to share, seek counsel, and confide in his wife. Some may say, "Well this was before Prophethood – once he started receiving regular revelation, he did not need to consult with anyone else", yet this is not the case either.

---

[72] Al-Bukhārī, *Ṣaḥīḥ al-Bukhārī*.

During the sixth year after Hijrah, the Muslims and Quraysh had just signed the Treaty of Ḥudaybiyyah. One of the conditions of the treaty was that the Muslims were to immediately return home to Medina and only undertake the pilgrimage the next year. This was difficult for some of the Companions ﷺ to accept, since they desperately hoped to perform the pilgrimage. When the Prophet ﷺ told the Companions ﷺ to get up, slaughter their sacrificial sheep and then shave their hair, they did not budge. He repeated his request to them three times, and still they remained in their places in hope that revelation from Allah ﷻ would bring about a change in circumstance. The Prophet ﷺ returned to his tent saddened by their refusal, and told Umm Salamah ﷺ what had happened. After considering his words, she said:

يَا نَبِيَّ اللَّهِ، أَتُحِبُّ ذلكَ؟ اخْرُجْ ثُمَّ لَا تُكَلِّمْ أَحَدًا مِنْهُمْ كَلِمَةً حَتَّى تَنْحَرَ بُدْنَكَ وَتَدْعُوَ حَالِقَكَ فَيَحْلِقَكَ

O Prophet of Allah, do you want them to do this? Then, go back out and do not utter a single word to any of them till you first slaughter your animals and shave your hair.[73]

The Prophet ﷺ applied this advice from his wife, and as expected, they all immediately rushed to do as he did.

Just as the example of Umm Salamah ﷺ demonstrates, there is a need for consultation and getting advice on both private and public issues, including even the greatest matters that affect society as a whole. To this end, consider the story of Prophet Mūsā ﷺ and how he came to be raised in the household of the Pharoah. Despite his disinterest and disregard for the new baby that his wife had found floating in a basket, she made the case for why this infant should be adopted into the household and raised by them, as is apparent in the following Qur'anic *āyah*:

[73] Al-Bukhārī, *Ṣaḥīḥ al-Bukhārī*.

وَقَالَتِ امْرَأَتُ فِرْعَوْنَ قُرَّتُ عَيْنٍ لِي وَلَكَ لَا تَقْتُلُوهُ عَسَى أَنْ يَنْفَعَنَا أَوْ نَتَّخِذَهُ وَلَدًا وَهُمْ لَا يَشْعُرُونَ

And the wife of Pharaoh said, "[He will be] a comfort of the eye for me and for you. Do not kill him; perhaps he may benefit us, or we may adopt him as a son." [74]

The Pharoah took his wife's advice. The gentle rationale and consultation of Āsiyah ﷺ with her husband caused the baby to grow up in the royal household of the most powerful man of the time. The outcome of this decision speaks for itself, as the story of Prophet Mūsā ﷺ and Pharoah is etched in history for all time.

After this same man grew up, Mūsā ﷺ came to a time in his life when he was exiled from his land and had no home, income, or plan for what his future may look like. After supplicating while taking shelter under the shade of a tree, Mūsā ﷺ observed two young women – among a group of boisterous men – struggling to take their flock to the water to drink. When he volunteered to do this for the sisters and they returned home to tell their father of what occurred, the eldest of the two offered this suggestion to her father:

يَا أَبَتِ اسْتَأْجِرْهُ إِنَّ خَيْرَ مَنِ اسْتَأْجَرْتَ الْقَوِيُّ الْأَمِينُ

One of the women said, "O my father, hire him. Indeed, the best one you can hire is the strong and the trustworthy." [75]

This suggestion was heeded by their father, who then approached Mūsā ﷺ to come to an agreement. This decision opened up the future of the Prophet Mūsā ﷺ. Not only did he find regular work for a fixed period, but he was married to the eldest of the two sisters, thus establishing himself and his family. The daughter's advice for her father to "hire him"

[74] *Al-Qaṣaṣ*, 28:9.

[75] *Al-Qaṣaṣ*, 28:26.

created a domino effect of goodness, and Ibn Mas'ūd 🕮 praised the young woman and future wife of Mūsā 🕮 as being gifted with strong intuition because of her counsel, saying: The people who had the most discernment were three: Abū Bakr's intuition about 'Umar; the companion of Yūsuf when he said, "Make his stay comfortable"; and the companion of Mūsā, when she said, "O my father, hire him. Indeed, the best one you can hire is the strong and the trustworthy."[76]

The benefit of mutual consultation

Psychologist and leading marriage researcher John Gottman and his colleagues studied 130 newlywed couples for six years to find what made marriages succeed and why. It turned out that happy, stable marriages all had one thing in common: *the husband was willing to accept his wife's influence.* In contrast, when husbands responded to their wives' complaints by stonewalling or belittling them, their marriages are bound to fail, More than four-fifths of those relationships studied – 81 percent – fell apart. That is an astounding statistic – and one worth paying attention to.

So, why would a man reject his wife's influence? There are plenty potential reasons for this. Perhaps the man grew up in a household where his own father never consulted his mother, and so this learned behaviour was passed to a new generation. Perhaps there is an underlying insecurity or social stigma that threatens a man's confidence if he is seen getting advice from his wife. Perhaps there is a stigma around men being "beta males" for not making all decisions independently without input from their wives. Of course, a man may simply fear a loss of power or being controlled, or worry that he is losing his role as a "leader" in the home.

---

[76] Ibn Kathīr, *Tafsīr Ibn Kathīr.*

The reality, ironically, is the polar opposite of this.

When a husband listens to his wife and accepts her influence, he is more likely to win the right and legitimacy to lead his wife and household. You are not "losing" your position by asking for and allowing input – you are strengthening it.

Though consultation and mutual buy-in are not necessary in every scenario, it is a generally positive culture to establish within the home. It is true that, in smaller matters, there may already be general mutual understandings that do not require exhaustive discussion, and in some other circumstances, husbands are expected to lead the family and have the final say. This becomes particularly important for matters that may get out of hand and can ruin a family. At all times, couples are to remember that they exist *together* in marriage, and therefore there are very few decisions that they make that do not directly affect their spouse. Therefore, in healthy marriages spouses consult each other and align themselves around each other's decisions and viewpoints.

In many unfortunate instances of unhealthy marriages, one of the two spouses has no access to the other's plans and may only glean limited information from other family members or even friends. These are imbalanced dynamics that – in many cases – result from mistrust and lack of respect for each other's judgement. If one or both partners are making unilateral decisions excessively, then, sooner or later, the relationship will suffer.

Similarly, try to ensure that you do not get involved in every single decision which can, in turn, become suffocating for your spouse. When it comes to the matters of the house, for example, a wife should be given autonomy, while men should be allowed to manage external affairs.

Finally, sisters must sincerely respect their husbands' opinions as much as is reasonable, as there is not anything more a husband needs than respect and trust that he can lead. As Dr. Emerson Eggerichs wisely expressed, "Respect does something to the soul of a man." If you are a wife, as obvious as it may sound, reassure your husband that you trust his leadership of your household, and are by his side as a supportive life partner.

Living with the same person day in and day out for the rest of your life brings many joys, but likewise brings challenges alongside them. No fair-minded person would want to spend their entire life with someone who is inflexible and does not care about their perspectives, so shared decision-making is a critical aspect of a successful long-term marriage.

Putting this principle into practice

1. Practice discussing an issue from both perspectives

There will be many situations that crop up during everyday life that you will disagree about. These matters could concern family, short-term plans, long-term goals, decisions around where you live, education options for your children, or work/study options for yourselves. Pick any issue that divides you and your spouse and come together with the intention of discussing the issue from both of your perspectives. This will require active listening and reflection on both sides. Allow your partner to honestly express themselves and do not interrupt or "correct" their perspective when they speak. Try to then summarise what you understood from their perspective and check with them that you have depicted it accurately. Then do the same for yourself. After this, speak about potential ways forward and the consequences of different options. Take this time to reassure and reaffirm your spouse that you are committed to the best outcome for the family, reminding your spouse that you are both on the same team.

2. Actively choose to concede on a present or future issue

When it comes to a current or future issue standing between you and your spouse, make a deliberate effort to put your spouse's perspective before your own. This is not to compromise on your own position, but merely to train yourself to accept the importance of your spouse's perspective. This will help you to truly understand what your spouse is feeling and will avoid situations where you may otherwise immediately shut out a point of view that differs from your own. This will crucially, foster an environment where consultation is more likely to happen. Make a list of five benefits from the perspective of your spouse that you would not have thought of otherwise, and use them to remind yourself why it is important to solicit the opinions of others. Finally, do not consider a matter too insignificant to consult on if it is important to your spouse. This display of respect can only increase your love and appreciation for one another.

CHAPTER SEVEN

On working together

وَتَعَاوَنُوا عَلَى ٱلْبِرِّ وَٱلتَّقْوَىٰ وَلَا تَعَاوَنُوا عَلَى ٱلْإِثْمِ وَٱلْعُدْوَٰنِ

Cooperate with one another in goodness and righteousness, and do not cooperate in sin and transgression.[77]

Working together is the cornerstone of a successful partnership and a way to elevate your relationship from mere survival to a deeply significant partnership.

One of the most effective methods to diffuse disputes and remind one another of the goodness in your relationship is a simple, yet drastically underrated intention: always work together as a *Muslim couple towards a common Islamic goal.*

More than one-third of husbands (39%) and wives (36%) cite "drifting apart" as the reason they divorced.[78] When many quarrelling, frustrated, and resentful couples are asked the question, "Do you engage in a joint Islamic activity of any sort?", the answer is always a firm "No." At first, many couples are not usually too impressed with this suggestion, or consider it irrelevant to their problems and issues with one another. However – like so many things in life – the benefits are often just under the surface, ready to be unearthed. So, how exactly

[77] *Al-Mā'idah*, 5:2.

[78] "Top Ten Key Facts on Marriage." Marriage Foundation. November 25 2023. https://marriagefoundation.org.uk/top-ten-key-facts-on-marriage/

would embarking on a joint Islamic activity possibly help your marriage to flourish?

1. It will establish an immovable rock of love in your relationship

Since our belief as Muslims is that Allah ﷻ is *al-Qawiyy* (the Most Powerful) and *al-Bāqī* (the Most Enduring), the logical conclusion is that a relationship centred on the Lord of such lofty attributes will also become the most powerful and most enduring relationship.

The Prophet ﷺ said:

ثَلَاثٌ مَنْ كُنَّ فِيهِ وَجَدَ حَلَاوَةَ الإِيمَانِ: أَنْ يَكُونَ اللهُ وَرَسُولُهُ أَحَبَّ إِلَيْهِ مِمَّا سِوَاهُمَا وَأَنْ يُحِبَّ المرْءَ لَا يُحِبُّهُ إِلَّا للهِ وَأَنْ يَكْرَهَ أَنْ يَعُودَ فِي الكُفْرِ بَعْدَ إِذْ أَنْقَذَهُ اللهُ مِنْهُ كَمَا يَكْرَهُ أَنْ يُلْقَى فِي النَّارِ

> There are three qualities that, whoever has them, will taste the sweetness of *īmān*: to love Allah and His Messenger more than anyone else; to love a person only for Allah's sake; and to hate returning to disbelief after Allah had saved him from it in the same way that he would hate to be thrown into the Fire.[79]

Why is it that when we talk about love for Allah's sake – the truest love – our minds automatically shift to our Muslim teachers, or perhaps to friends who attend the same study circle in the masjid? Have you not considered that you can love your spouse for Allah's sake as well? Unlike love that is founded exclusively on carnal desires or having children, love for Allah's sake is the strongest anchor as it is set upon the Most Powerful ﷻ Himself.

[79] Al-Bukhārī, *Ṣaḥīḥ al-Bukhārī;* Muslim, *Ṣaḥīḥ Muslim.*

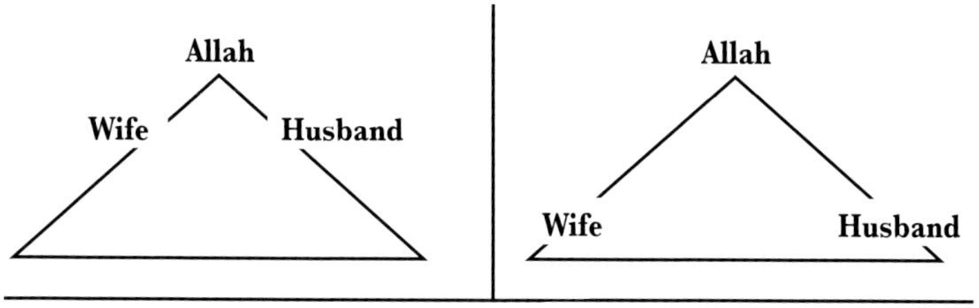

As a rule, the distance between Allah and a couple is proportional to the distance between the spouses themselves. Evidently, the closer the spouses draw to Allah ﷻ, the nearer they will be drawn to one another.

The more you endeavour to bring Islam into your relationship, the more you will love each other for the sake of Allah ﷻ. The more you love each other for His sake, the closer you will become.

2. It will eliminate pettiness from your lives

There is often a very strong correlation between couples who do not perform any joint Islamic activity or share higher ambitions but fight and quarrel over petty matters. In fact, such couples are too embarrassed to even share their problems with a counsellor due to how petty it sounds – that is, if they can even remember them in the first place!

Since the couple have not spent their time in noble affairs, Shayṭān keeps them busy with trivial circumstances instead. As for couples who have invited Islam into their daily or weekly schedules, whose minds and priorities have risen to new heights that transcend this world and rise into the Hereafter, they find themselves far too busy to be slowed down or hurt by petty things. Projects that remind you of the greater purpose of life also ensure that you can distinguish what really matters and what is not worth your attention.

3. Your spouse will be the most attractive person to you

A Moroccan brother relating his journey to repentance mentioned how he was raised in an upper-class family, only ever mixing with the elite. According to him, beauty was – somehow – far more prevalent in their midst. He said:

After I found my way back to Allah ﷻ, I began to search for marriage, but because of my background, my eye had become accustomed to certain standards. I made so much *duʿāʾ* for a wife of very specific characteristics. Each time I did *ʿumrah*, drank Zamzam water, or was in prostration, my hands would instinctively rise in supplication, earnestly articulating my unwavering desire. Years passed by and my *duʿāʾ* did not change one bit, until the day came when Allah ﷻ would send the very mirror reflection of my *duʿāʾ* to the home of my parents, after which we were married.

He continued:

As I was asleep one night, I fleetingly stirred, shifting from one side to another, only to catch a glimpse of my wife, who stood resolute in the heart of our room, enveloped in the folds of her hijab. There, in the darkness, she stood in voluntary night prayer. I had no idea that this was her habit. Although it was only a brief snapshot in my eyes before I fell back to sleep, the image of her standing in prayer was etched onto my mind forever. As a result, whenever I would witness beauty that my lower insinuations suggested may exceed the beauty of my wife, this image of her in prayer at night would appear before me, and at once I would remember that I have the most beautiful woman in the world.

4. It will ease the intensity of the interrogation within the court of Allah

Except for a select and blessed minority, most Muslims will not be granted Paradise until they first provide satisfactory answers to a series of questions within the court of Allah ﷻ on the Day of Reckoning. No one can claim to be caught off guard on that Day, because these questions have been fully conveyed by the Prophet ﷺ so that we can make full preparations for them. One of these questions relates to family.

The Prophet ﷺ said:

إِنَّ اللَّهَ سَائِلٌ كُلَّ رَاعٍ عَمَّا اسْتَرْعَاهُ، أَحَفِظَ ذَلِكَ أَمْ ضَيَّعَ ؟ حَتَّى يُسْأَلَ الرَّجُلُ عَلَى أَهْلِ بَيْتِهِ

Allah is going to ask each shepherd about his flock, whether he upheld this trust or abused it, until a man will be asked about his household.[80]

The Prophet ﷺ said:

لَيَلْقَيَنَّ أَحَدُكُمْ رَبَّهُ يَوْمَ القِيَامَةِ فَيَقُولُ لَهُ: أَلَمْ أُسَخِّرْ لَكَ الخَيْلَ وَالإِبِلَ؟ أَلَمْ أَذَرْكَ تَرْأَسُ وَتَرْبَعُ؟ أَلَمْ أُزَوِّجْكَ فُلَانَةَ خَطَبَهَا الخُطَّابُ فَمَنَعْتُهُمْ وَزَوَّجْتُكَ

One of you will meet his Lord on the Day of Judgement and He will say to him, "Did I not give you horses and camels? Did I not give you authority? Did I not marry you to so and so, although others had asked for her hand, but I kept them away and married her to you?"[81]

Adopting joint Islamic habits and rituals is undoubtedly a means of easing the intensity of this upcoming interrogation in the Court of Allah ﷻ.

[80] Al-Bukhārī, *Ṣaḥīḥ al-Bukhārī;* Muslim, *Ṣaḥīḥ Muslim.*
[81] Muslim, *Ṣaḥīḥ Muslim.*

5. It will become the reason for your joint entry to Jannah

The couple that make an active effort today in coming together for the pleasure of Allah ﷻ, the couple who worked together for His sake will be blessed by the Angels on the Day of Judgement, who will usher them together into Paradise.

Allah ﷻ said:

إِنَّ أَصْحَابَ الْجَنَّةِ الْيَوْمَ فِي شُغُلٍ فَاكِهُونَ. هُمْ وَأَزْوَاجُهُمْ فِي ظِلَالٍ عَلَى الْأَرَائِكِ مُتَّكِئُونَ

Indeed, the companions of Paradise, that Day, will be amused in joyful occupation. They and their spouses in shade, reclining on adorned thrones.[82]

Putting this principle into practice

Many couples eventually come to love the idea of working together towards a common Islamic goal, realising the extent to which they had suffocated their relationship by not doing this. So, the question that usually follows is: what does a joint Islamic activity look like? Below are a few suggestions that have proven to be transformative methods to awaken love and readmit mercy back into marriages.

Children

Raising righteous children is the ultimate objective of a couple, and children should never be seen or treated as a mere by-product of a marriage. Children are the ultimate "joint project" for which you both must consciously plan and ask yourselves important questions. How will we nurture this child and raise a righteous Muslim? How will we equip them with the skills to navigate the challenges of life and hold onto their faith? What steps must we take now, what skills must we learn, what knowl-

[82] *Yā Sīn*, 36:55-56.

edge must we acquire, what books must we read, and which study circles must we attend? These are questions that should be considered even before your baby is conceived and will continue throughout your lives as parents. While this continues, we also need to invest in other short-term projects.

A weekly outing to the local masjid to attend a class

A friend of mine told me that one of the most wonderful phases in his Islamic life, for both him and his spouse, was their drive to their local mosque to attend a weekly class. Afterwards, they would dine at a local restaurant and ponder over what had inspired them and share their notes. He said that he and his spouse made a date out of it and were at their happiest on those days.

Even if you need to drive a little further out, it is worth the investment. Do not be afraid of asking your family to look after the children for a few hours each week (and find a way of returning the favour) so you can spend productive hours with your spouse.

A movie night

Consult people whom you trust to create a playlist of engaging, light, and heart-softening Islamic or otherwise beneficial video content. Create such a playlist that will last you for 6 months at a pace of two videos a week, for example.

Two units of joint prayer before you sleep

Make a habit of praying together at night, but start with something manageable, like two units that you carry out together after your 'Ishā' prayer (and the Sunnah prayer that follows it) and before your Witr prayer. The Prophet ﷺ said:

رَحِمَ اللهُ رَجُلًا قَامَ مِنَ اللَّيْلِ فَصَلَّى وَأَيْقَظَ امْرَأَتَهُ فَإِنْ أَبَتْ نَضَحَ فِي
وَجْهِهَا الْمَاءَ، رَحِمَ اللهُ امْرَأَةً قَامَتْ مِنَ اللَّيْلِ فَصَلَّتْ وَأَيْقَظَتْ زَوْجَهَا
فَإِنْ أَبَى نَضَحَتْ فِي وَجْهِهِ الْمَاءَ

May Allah have mercy upon a man who gets up at night to pray, then wakes his wife to pray, but if she refuses, he sprinkles water in her face. May Allah have mercy on a woman who gets up at night to pray, then wakes her husband to pray, and if he refuses, she sprinkles water in his face.[83]

Couples are quick to argue that mercy is missing in their relationship, but are very slow in doing what is required to bring it back. Here, the Prophet ﷺ makes *du'ā'* that mercy enters the lives of couples who pray at night, and his *du'ā'* is not rejected.

Ramadan fasts that need making up

Most women will have accumulated days of Ramadan that need to be made up, and require encouragement to do so. This can be converted into a marriage investment opportunity by making an intention to fast together as a couple every sunnah day – Monday and Thursday – or whenever possible. According to the Prophet ﷺ, there are two forms of happiness that the fasting person experiences, one of which is during the breaking of the fast. How many opportunities for happiness do couples miss out on when it comes to this weekly opportunity for bonding? Make sure you do not neglect to schedule these fasts together!

Husband and wife reading club

Create a reading list for just you and your wife. Populate the list with both Islamic books and beneficial mainstream reads. Endeavour to complete one book a month. Whether you are

[83] Abū Dāwūd, *Sunan Abū Dāwūd*.

shopping or taking a walk, or just milling around the house, you will never be short of interesting conversation topics that many couples complain they lack. Furthermore, this activity nurtures listening skills and paves a solid pathway to expressing views and interests, which are dangerously absent in many marriages.

Design a joint Islamic project together

Henry Ford once said, "Coming together is a beginning. Keeping together is progress. Working together is success."[84]

A project reveals our expectations and our deepest desires. It is a reflection of our personality and aspirations. What a shame it would be to need to search for someone else to share that with because you and your spouse do not have this type of conversation.

It is not necessary to have all the same dreams as one's spouse; however, it is necessary to know of each other's dreams and to talk about them with each other, to be able to respect them, and sometimes even to get on board with them. These are valuable moments of intimate discussion that should happen primarily between husband and wife.

When you are both goal-oriented, your mistakes seem smaller, your quarrels are fewer, your lines of communication are wider, your sense of unity is clearer, your marriage satisfaction is greater, and your bond is immeasurably stronger. This bond is bound to weaken if you are both constantly working apart from each other.

Your joint Islamic project could be to select and complete the study of one Islamic text together, to memorise the entire Qur'an with an *ijāzah* (license) in *tajwīd* (Qur'anic elocution)

[84] "27 Great Quotes." Jmark. November 25 2023. https://www.jmark.com/27-great-quotes-teamwork-inspire-jmark-hope-will-inspire/

within five years, to understand 90% of Qur'anic Arabic within two years, to establish a *tajwīd* institute or educational foundation, to work with existing institutions and add value to their work, to volunteer at charities or community groups, or to raise funds for students of sacred knowledge. As long as your intentions are grounded in Allah's pleasure, there are a myriad of opportunities ahead of you.

Start a frank conversation about your goal from as early as now. Pinpoint your strengths, brainstorm ideas, consult other teachers and families, and find your common goal. Do this for the sake of Allah ﷻ, then for the sake of the Hereafter, and then for the sake of your marriage.

Though all these examples are joint Islamic activities, you should not neglect the recreational activities spouses can do together. In fact, the occasional joint recreational activity with your spouse will improve the experience of working together Islamically. Recreational companionship is one of the most common love needs, and also one of the best divorce-proofing strategies. Too many spouses check-out of their marriages because they become attracted to someone else who shares their interest at work or in a particular hobby. Being able to share a recreational interest helps protect your affections from being drawn to others. Enjoying recreational time together will also allow you to laugh together and see the soft, carefree side of each other again. When the responsibilities of life are heavy, it is often easy to forget the joy, humour, and playfulness you once shared with your spouse. Activities such as these will inject some much-needed levity back into your relationship dynamic.

CHAPTER EIGHT

On honourable treatment

وَعَاشِرُوهُنَّ بِالْمَعْرُوفِ

And live with them in kindness (or fairly).[85]

Treating your spouse in a kind, fair and honourable manner seems such an obvious aspect of marriage – why would it warrant an entire chapter to explain it at all? And why, by extension, does it seem so sorely missing within marital relationships? The instruction in this verse to "live with them" uses the word *ʿāshirūhunna*, which encompasses so much more than can be rendered in translation. Here we will examine this Qur'anic concept and explore how it can be applied practically to strengthen the bonds of love within marriage.

The word *ʿashara* in Arabic signifies perfection and completeness. The word ʿashīrah, or tribe, is derived from it, as a tribe is a collection of people whose affairs are complete and so is their ability to dominate others. Similarly, the word *ʿasharah* refers to the complete number ten. In fact, the number ten is commonly used in rating systems across the world to evaluate and rate various things, such as movies, products, services and

[85] *Al-Nisāʾ*, 4:19.

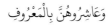

performances, with ten often being the highest score and an indication of excellence or perfection.

So, the instruction in this verse, which states that to "live with them" uses the term *ʿāshirūhunna*, which therefore refers to a treatment that is wholesome, complete and of the highest form.

So profound is this Qur'anic principle of *ʿāshirūhunna bi al-maʿrūf* (and live with them in kindness) that the Prophet Muhammad ﷺ took the opportunity during the greatest gathering witnessed by humanity – his farewell sermon on thc day of ʿArafah – to emphasise it, enjoining tens of thousands of his followers to "fear Allah concerning women, for you have taken them on the security of Allah and have made their persons lawful unto you by the words of Allah."[86]

Commenting on this Qur'anic principle, the great Qur'anic exegete Abū Bakr al-Jaṣṣāṣ al-Ḥanafī رحمه الله wrote:

أَمَرَ لِلْأَزْوَاجِ بِعِشْرَةِ نِسَائِهِمْ بِالمَعْرُوفِ وَمِنَ المَعْرُوفِ أَنْ يُوَفِيَهَا حَقَّهَا مِنَ المَهْرِ وَالنَّفَقَةِ والَقَسْمِ وَتَرْكِ أَذَاهَا بالكَلَام الغَلِيظِ وَالإِعْرَاضِ عَنْهَا والمَيْلِ إِلَى غَيْرِهَا وَتَرْكِ العَبُوسِ وَالقُطُوبِ فِي وَجْهِهَا بِغَيْرِ ذَنْبٍ.

> It is an instruction to spouses to treat their wives with kindness, and kindness includes fulfilling their rights regarding dowry, financial support, fair division of time and resources, refraining from using hurtful speech, avoiding neglect or showing interest in others, and refraining from frowning or showing displeasure towards them without a justifiable reason.[87]

As for the latter part of this Qur'anic principle, "and live with them in kindness (or fairly)", the word *maʿrūf* (translated as kindness/fairly) shares a linguistic root with the word *ʿurf*, which refers to customs and norms. Islam gives weight to the customary practices of a people on the condition that they do

[86] Muslim, *Ṣaḥīḥ Muslim*.
[87] Al-Jaṣṣāṣ, *Aḥkām al-Qur'ān*.

not oppose a matter of the religion.

Norms and customs vary from community to community, and with Islam being the fluid, encompassing, and timeless religion that it is, believers are encouraged to align their affairs with the norms of their society in many matters. What could this potentially mean for marriage? Expectations of how kind treatment ought to be shown vary according to time, place, and culture, although a few foundational principles are certainly universal. The *maʿrūf* must be understood and practised according to the norms of the culture that the couple were raised in. The Qur'an contains further injunctions to adhere to customary understandings of goodness.

With respect to rights between the spouses, Allah ﷻ said:

وَلَهُنَّ مِثْلُ الَّذِي عَلَيْهِنَّ بِالْمَعْرُوفِ

And women have rights equal to their obligations in kindness.[88]

With respect to the rights of a child, Allah ﷻ said:

وَعَلَى الْمَوْلُودِ لَهُ رِزْقُهُنَّ وَكِسْوَتُهُنَّ بِالْمَعْرُوفِ

The child's father will provide maintenance and clothing for the mother during that period in kindness.[89]

This is because the expenditures and expectations of the wealthy differ from that of average or less affluent families.

With respect to the etiquettes of divorce, Allah ﷻ said:

الطَّلَاقُ مَرَّتَانِ فَإِمْسَاكٌ بِمَعْرُوفٍ أَوْ تَسْرِيحٌ بِإِحْسَانٍ

Divorce may be retracted twice, then the husband must either retain his wife in kindness or separate from her with grace.[90]

---

[88] *Al-Baqarah*, 2:228.
[89] *Al-Baqarah*, 2:233.
[90] *Al-Baqarah*, 2:229.

So, bringing ourselves back to the principle in question – "live with them in kindness" – whilst there are constants in the religion that are not to be compromised on, there are also customary expectations in the marital experience that the religion expects one to uphold. For example, if you have married a woman from an upper-class family whose parents did not expect her to lift a finger, then you should be aware of what this means. She may never have made a bed, never cooked a meal in her life, and had maids doing everything for her. That is something that a husband will need to accommodate for, particularly in certain societies where hiring maids is a cultural norm.

Putting this principle into practice

What are some of the expectations of the modern-day woman, the *maʿrūf* expected by many wives today? Though both women and men should treat each other with maʿrūf, the following topics specifically address how husbands may treat their wives with maʿrūf.

Household chores

In a recent survey conducted by a matrimonial website, 51.9% of women said that they want their prospective spouses to help with household chores, while 39.5% want a husband with culinary skills.

Aesthetic care

It may have been perfectly normal in the past that husbands did not make any efforts towards their physical appearance or even practice basic grooming. However, things have changed significantly in this regard – for better or worse – when it comes to expectations of the husband and wife alike. Men are expected to make an effort to not only be clean, presentable and well-groomed, but also to keep in shape and remain fit and strong. Just as women are expected to maintain themselves when it comes to looking after their appearance, wearing attractive clothing, and beautifying themselves at home, men ought to do the same. Doing so can and does make an impact on your wife, as you not only give her something pleasurable to look at, but signal that she is worth making the effort for. This is evident in the following statement of Ibn ʿAbbās ﵄:

إِنِّي لَأُحِبُّ أَنْ أَتَزَيَّنَ لِلْمَرْأَةِ كَمَا أُحِبُّ أَنْ تَتَزَيَّنَ لِي الْمَرْأَةُ لِأَنَّ اللهَ يَقُولُ:
(وَلَهُنَّ مِثْلُ الَّذِي عَلَيْهِنَّ بِالْمَعْرُوفِ)

I like to adorn myself for my wife just as I like her to adorn herself for me, because Allah said, "And they (the women) have [rights] like [the obligations] they are under according to what is maʿrūf."[91]

Similarly, Muhammad ibn al-Ḥusayn ﵀ used to wear expensive clothes and explained why he did so by saying:

إِنَّ لِي نِسَاءً وَجِوارِيَ فَأُزَيِّنُ نَفْسِي كَيْ لَا يَنْظُرْنَ إِلَى غَيْرِي

I adorn myself for my women so that they do not look towards others.

The same way you want your wife to be sensual, alluring, and with an aura of femininity, she also wants a husband who is well-polished and presentable, and doing so constitutes living with her in *maʿrūf*.

Meaningful talk

There may have been a time when husbands would not speak much with their wives, and if they did, it would be little more

[91] Al-Bayhaqī, *Al-Sunan al-Kubrā li al-Bayhaqī.*

than briefly checking in on their children and households, talking out loud about their job, and perhaps even commenting on the weather if they were really struggling! Today, there is an expectation to engage in real talk, as deep and real conversations are the "glue" that will hold you together and create the emotional intimacy married people yearn for.

Me time

In the past, perhaps it was expected from women that they would silently and constantly graft for their family without a moment's respite. Today, however, the desire is that women are given "me" time. No matter how supportive a woman's husband and in-laws are, she always needs some time to herself. Wives need time to evaluate themselves, catalogue the thoughts that have been running through their minds, sort through the issues that have been weighing down on them, and get a fresh outlook for the future. Taking a short break from her responsibilities to recharge as a person and not just a mother or a wife is important to keep a woman feeling on top of things. Having enough downtime is a necessity to cope with difficulties and thrive in life, as nobody can pour from an empty cup. A rested, fulfilled wife will have more to give her husband and household.

Creating friendships

It is not feasible to merely seek romantic fulfilment from our partners – we also need them to be a best friend, counterpart, therapist and co-parent. However, with these increased expectations come increased rates of dissatisfaction, as couples struggle to keep up with the many demands placed upon them. So how do you manage these heightened expectations around marriage? To begin, you should consciously try to alleviate the pressure for your partner to "do it all". Research indicates that people with access to more social resources (meaning a larger support system) tend to have more successful marriages. Facilitate this for your spouse and allow them to find multiple outlets to "decompress" and find solace in good friends, family, and community.

Romance

Husbands of the pasts were perhaps only ever expected to come home with an income and shopping bags. There may have been a time where husbands were not expected to bring home flowers, chocolates or personalised gifts from time to time, nor to take the family on regular holidays. A woman's presence was a given, such that there was an idea that "she isn't going anywhere." This has radically shifted in our times, as women have a cultural expectation to be made to feel special, cherished, and romantically fulfilled by their spouses. Romance requires effort, and it is not always about great or grand gestures, but consistent attention and concern. Take time to pay attention to the things that your spouse truly appreciates and respond to her cues. Romance looks different for every couple, so make an effort to learn what your spouse really appreciates from you in this regard.

Domestic violence

A shocking reality that collides head-on with this principle is that of domestic violence. One out of three women will be abused in their lifetime by an intimate partner. This staggering statistic applies across all races, religions, and nationalities. This violence conducted by spouses and intimate partners leads to, on average, two women are murdered each week in Britain.[92] According to new research, women who have experienced

92 "Understanding Abuse Statistics." Living Without Abuse. November 25 2023. https://lwa.org.uk/understanding-abuse/statistics/

domestic abuse have three times the risk of developing a mental illness, including severe conditions such as schizophrenia and bipolar disorder, compared with those who have not experienced abuse. The impact of growing up in a home with domestic violence has catastrophic and long-term consequences for children too, often creating lifelong trauma and dysfunctional behaviour patterns.

ʿĀ'ishah ﵂ narrates how domestic violence was not the way of the Prophet ﷺ:

ما ضَرَبَ رَسُولُ اللهِ صَلَّى اللهُ عَلَيْهِ وَسَلَّمَ شَيْئًا قَطُّ بِيَدِهِ وَلَا امْرَأَةً وَلَا خَادِمًا إِلَّا أَنْ يُجَاهِدَ فِي سَبِيلِ اللهِ

The Prophet Muhammad ﷺ never struck anything with his hand – neither a woman nor a servant. His only strike was when engaged in fighting for the sake of Allah.[93]

Similarly, when a group of women came to the home of the Prophet ﷺ complaining about the harshness of their husbands, the Prophet ﷺ announced:

لَقَدْ أَطَافَ بِآلِ مُحَمَّدٍ نِسَاءٌ كَثِيرٌ يَشْكُونَ أَزْوَاجَهُنَّ، لَيْسَ أُولَئِكَ بِخِيَارِكُمْ

Many women from the household of Muhammad have come complaining about their husbands. They are not the best among you.[94]

Indeed, the Prophet Muhammad ﷺ would discourage women from marrying certain men if he was aware of them being violent towards women. When Fāṭimah bint Qays ﵂ consulted the Prophet Muhammad ﷺ about potential suitors who had proposed to her, he said,

[93] Muslim, *Ṣaḥīḥ Muslim.*

[94] Abū Dāwūd, *Sunan Abū Dāwūd.*

أَمَّا مُعَاوِيَةُ فَرَجُلٌ تَرِبٌ لَا مَالَ لَهُ وَأَمَّا أَبُو جَهْمٍ فَرَجُلٌ ضَرَّابٌ لِلنِّسَاءِ
وَلَكِنْ أُسَامَةُ بْنُ زَيْدٍ

As for Muʿāwiyah, he is poor. As for Abū Jahm, he is a woman beater. Marry Usāmah ibn Zayd.[95]

Men: *Do not* delay your application of this principle

Embracing this principle and nurturing your marriage through tenderness is a valuable investment – not only in your relationship, but also in yourself. Compare marriage to a bank account: the more you invest in it, the more you can reap its benefits. Just as is the case with your finances, when the time comes to face challenges or withdraw from the relationship, having built a solid foundation of deposits through love and kindness ensures that the relationship can continue to flourish another day. However, if you constantly withdraw without making any deposits, you will eventually find yourself in a deficit, unable to sustain the relationship – you cannot take unless you also give. At this point, spouses may struggle to cope with each other, lacking the reserves to rely on. Unfortunately, it can be difficult to recover when you have accumulated significant debts and have depleted your partner's goodwill, thus pushing the relationship to a juncture beyond repair.

Women: *Do not* abuse this principle

On the flip side of this principle is the reality of double standards and contradictory expectations that may be held by some of our Muslim sisters when it comes to marriage. Many self-identifying Muslim feminists mix the contradictory ideals of 50/50 marital expectations with the Islamic expectation to be fully financially provided for. This creates a Frankenstein outcome that oppresses both parties within the dynamics.

[95] Muslim, *Ṣaḥīḥ Muslim*.

Some may argue that a feminist, in the true sense, is one who aspires for an equal division across all responsibilities, finances, household chores, child rearing duties, etc. Naturally, this would mean a right of only half of your husband's resources, half of his time with children, and perhaps half of his protection in dangerous situations. It is inconsistent for Muslim women to therefore expect equally shared domestic responsibilities which is promoted by strictly egalitarian feminists, while claiming 100% of her rights as a Muslim woman.

A situation where a woman demands all the traditional benefits of a Muslim marriage but denounces the traditional responsibilities is an unfair one. While she may want a strong and decisive husband, a chivalrous man who can be a rock to lean on, a mature and romantic charmer, and a protector who will work three jobs in the process of providing for her, when it comes to her responsibilities, she may hesitate to do her duty. In the same breath, some of them will say, "Don't expect me to maintain a home, I am not under any duty to see you as the leader of the household, you do not get to tell me to do this – but pay my bills because Islam says that you must!"

This unbalanced sense of entitlement needs to be called out. A Muslim man who performs all the traditional functions of an Islamic marriage will aspire for a woman who will perform her traditional function as a wife. This is consistent and fair.

CHAPTER NINE

On just leadership

الرِّجَالُ قَوَّامُونَ عَلَى النِّسَاءِ

Men are the protectors and maintainers of women.[96]

Both men and women are Allah's honoured creations, and Allah ﷻ would never oppress any of His creatures. Allah ﷻ prepares each of His servants to fulfil the purpose that He intends for them, bestowing upon them the innate abilities needed to carry out that purpose.

Allah ﷻ has given women the exclusive qualities of being able to fall pregnant, bear children, and nurse them. This is a blessed and taxing responsibility, which Allah ﷻ prepares women for physically, mentally, and emotionally. On this basis, it is only just that Allah ﷻ would give different responsibilities to men, the other half of humanity, to complement her role. Men are tasked with fulfilling the needs of those women, protecting them, and providing for them, and as such, Allah ﷻ bestows upon men the innate physical, mental, and emotional qualities that would allow them to excel in doing what is required of them.

Every institution has a natural need for leadership, whereby leaders ensure that the interest of every member is fulfilled. The institution of marriage is no different, and the "leader" of

[96] *Al-Nisā'*, 4:34.

this relationship, as appointed by Allah ﷻ, is the husband. He has been put in a position of authority and care for his wife, and no similar obligation is applied to the wife.

In fact, in the English language, the etymological origin of the word "husband" is from "house band", which means a person who holds the house together. The role of the husband in a marriage was always the protector or guardian of the house, and naturally, this position comes with its privileges and responsibilities. The Prophet g spoke of this natural hierarchy:

كلكم رَاعٍ وَكُلُّكُمْ مَسْؤُولٌ عَنْ رَعِيَّتِهِ وَالأَمِيرُ رَاعٍ والرَّجُلُ رَاعٍ عَلَى أَهْلِ بَيتِهِ وَالمَرْأَةُ رَاعِيَةٌ عَلَى بَيْتِ زَوْجها وَوَلَدِهِ فَكُلُّكُمْ رَاعٍ، وَكُلُّكُمْ مَسْؤُولٌ عَنْ رَعِيَّتِه

All of you are shepherds, and each one is responsible for their flock. The ruler is a shepherd, and the man is a shepherd over his household, and the woman is a shepherd over her house and children. So, all of you are shepherds, and each one is responsible for their flock.[97]

What does it mean that men are "protectors and maintainers" of women? To truly understand this term, let us examine the Arabic words translated as "protectors and maintainers". This word is qawwāmūn, the plural of qawwām. This word – qawwām – in turn, is an emphatic form of the word qayyim, which means a person who manages the affairs of others. Within the context of a family, the qayyim of a woman can be her husband, guardian, or whoever is entrusted with her care and well-being. This includes ensuring that her needs are met and that the household is rooted in Islamic principles, upholding the rights and commandments of Allah ﷻ.

To qualify for this role, a man is required to use wisdom, maturity, knowledge, careful deliberation, emotional intelligence,

[97] Al-Bukhārī, *Ṣaḥīḥ al-Bukhārī;* Muslim, *Ṣaḥīḥ Muslim.*

and exercises pardon and patience. It means that he cannot be hasty and offhand with his decisions. It is not an invitation to disregard his wife's opinions, suppress her individuality or negate her identity. Hence the primary role of the husband is to be a leader in goodness, which includes his spending on his family, while the primary role of the wife is to provide encouragement, support, and respect.

How the Prophet ﷺ put this duty into practice?

The Prophet ﷺ did not behave like an emperor who lorded over his family. When we carefully ponder on his blessed life, we find the most profound testimony of the fact that a man's protection and maintenance of women in no way entails unreasonableness, compulsion, or subjugation.

ʿĀ'ishah ﵂ was asked, "What did the Prophet ﷺ do in the house?" She replied:

كَانَ يَكُونُ فِي مِهْنَةِ أَهْلِهِ فَإِذَا سَمِعَ الأَذَانَ خَرَجَ

He used to be engaged in household chores, and when he heard the call to prayer, he would go out.[98]

Similarly, a man asked ʿĀ'ishah ﵂, "Did the Prophet ﷺ do any work in his house?" She replied:

نَعَمْ، كَانَ رَسُولُ اللهِ صَلَّى اللهُ عَلَيْهِ وَسَلَّمَ يَخْصِفُ نَعلَهُ وَيَخِيطُ ثَوبَهُ وَيَعْمَلُ فِي بَيْتِهِ كَمَا يَعْمَلُ أَحَدُكُمْ فِي بَيْتِهِ.

Yes, the Messenger of Allah ﷺ used to mend his sandals, sew his garments, and engage in household work just as any one of you does in his own house.[99]

[98] Muslim, *Ṣaḥīḥ Muslim*.
[99] Al-Bukhārī, *Ṣaḥīḥ al-Bukhārī*.

What about role reversal?

Financial realities often dictate that a single person cannot provide all the expenses for the household alone and the wife must work to contribute to running costs. Islamically, this is considered an additional responsibility a wife has taken on, until her husband is able to make ends meet. In other harmful cases, there may be no financial need at all, yet men choose to stay at home voluntarily and allow their wives to take on financial responsibility for the household.

Harvard University researcher Professor Alexandra Killewald analysed data on the lives, marriages and finances of 6,300 couples, including 1,700 who had divorced. It was found that couples are more likely to divorce when the man does not work full-time.[100]

The sad truth is that being a stay-at-home dad can have a damaging effect on relationships, as divorce lawyer Vanessa Lloyd Platt has witnessed. Divorces where the man is a full-time dad have doubled in the last five years, and now account for 10% of all marital break-ups. Fiona Macrae, writing for the Daily Mail, reported on her findings as such:

"In my experience, 25-30% of couples where there is a stay-at-home dad end in acrimonious splits – and it is almost always the woman who initiates proceedings", she says. "It is the biggest explosion we've seen this year. It is absolutely astounding. The bottom line is, they do not respect their other half any more. If they do not respect him, they do not fancy him – and it is a slippery slope." There are knock on effects to this role reversal, when men stay at home and women interact with

[100] Fiona Macrae, "The REAL Reason Modern Marriages End." The Daily Mail. November 25 2023. https://www.dailymail.co.uk/sciencetech/article-3710922/The-REAL-reason-modern-marriages-end-Women-likely-divorce-stay-home-dads-fail-live-breadwinner-stereotype.html

high-achieving successful male colleagues who seem to embody all the strong masculine traits lacking within her house-husband. "What we're seeing here is not just a reversal but a total revolution in gender roles."[101]

In Sweden, which ranks first in the EU's gender equality index, economists recently studied how promotions to top jobs affected the probability of divorce for each gender. The result: women were much more likely to pay a higher personal price for their career success. "Promotion to a top job in politics increases the divorce rate of women but not for men, and women who become CEOs divorce faster than men who become CEOs," according to Johanna Rickne, a professor at Stockholm University and co-author of research on the link between family finances and divorce.

In recent times, we've also seen the rise of the "tradwives" movement, which is gaining thousands of followers in countries as diverse as the UK, Brazil, Germany, and Japan. "The movement's rising because women have had enough of feminism in the UK and elsewhere", claims Dixie Andelin Forsyth, talking about the surprise resurgence of interest in her mother's 1963 book, Fascinating Womanhood. "We say to feminists: thanks for the trousers, but we see life a different way."

Central to #tradwifehood's message is the notion that feminism, with its questioning of "traditional" sex roles, has gone too far. "Tell men not to be men and women not to be women and you get family breakdown," writes a tradwife named Jade. "I simply think the old ways were better: when men provided and protected, and women took care of their men. I just ask not to be judged."

101 Martin Daubney, "Why Being a Stay at Home Dad is the Quickest Way to Kill your Sex Life." The Daily Mail. November 25 2023. https://www.dailymail.co.uk/femail/article-2182970/Why-stay-home-dad-quickest-way-kill-sex-life-lead-wives-stray.html

Written by Helen Andelin, an American Mormon mother of eight, Fascinating Womanhood argues that women should aspire towards an ideal of femininity, manage men with their "feminine charms", and see wifeliness as the foundation of a happy marriage. In a sign of the renewed interest in 'trad' femininity, Fascinating Womanhood, now a teaching business run by Andelin's daughter Dixie Andelin Forsyth, has relaunched the movement's 1970s "femininity classes" as both real-world and online courses. Over 100,000 women are signed up to these classes worldwide, including hundreds of women in the UK.[102]

Suzanne Venker – bestselling author of *The Alpha Females Guide to Men and Marriage, The Bossy Wife Diet, The Two Income Trap, and America is in Love with the Alpha Female* speaks of the appearance of the alpha woman, saying, "She's the quintessential modern woman – assertive, razor-sharp, and fully in control. Her success in the marketplace is undeniable, a downright boon to society. But what happens when the alpha woman gets married? She becomes an alpha wife, of course. An alpha wife is in charge of everything and everyone. She is, quite simply, the boss. The problem is, no man wants a boss for a wife. That type of relationship may work for a spell, but it will eventually come crashing down."

Since 1970, as women became more powerful outside the home and became more "alpha" within it, the divorce rate has quadrupled – and it is women who lead the charge. Today, 70% of divorces are initiated by wives. Do men just make lousy husbands? Not at that rate, says Venker, who writes: The truth is that women weren't raised to be wives. No one told them

[102] Sally Howards, "'I want to Submit to my Husband like a 50s Housewife': inside the Controversial UK Tradwife Movement." Stylist. November 25 2023. https://www.stylist.co.uk/long-reads/traditional-1950s-housewife-tradwife-tradlife-explained-women-reject-feminism-careers-domestic-housework/315360

their real power lies in their femininity. You're going to have to become a beta at home. Do whatever you want in your day job (whether you're employed or at home raising kids), but you're going to have to switch gears at 5 o'clock. If you do not, your marriage will continue to be one giant fight. Women are taught to chuck their femininity and to become more like men: dominant, aggressive, and in charge. That may get you ahead at work. But at home, it will land you in a ditch.

Laura Doyle, author of *The Surrendered Wife* and a later edition entitled *The Empowered Wife*, and has become a household name in America. She claims she ended years of loneliness and misery in her marriage by a simple process. She stopped treating her husband John like a child and telling him what to wear and what to do. She stopped criticising and nagging, handed over the finances to him, and made herself always available. As a result, "The man who had wooed me was back."

Doyle continues, writing, "Surrendering does not mean being a doormat; it means relinquishing inappropriate control. Control is the enemy of intimacy. If you try to control your husband, you end up emasculating him. He sees you as his mother, and which man wants to have sex with his mother? Marriages work best when you let the man be the man and you let him take appropriate control."

Doyle's caveat – ignored by her critics – is that if you are with someone who is violent, an addict, or a serial adulterer, not only should you not surrender, but you should also leave the relationship quickly.

Surrendering has struck a chord with many women who do not desire to control their husbands and, as a result, her book is an international bestseller, and her days are packed with engagements presenting her ideas to new audiences.

The truth is, many women are not fully aware of the type of power and influence they can have over their husbands if they resist the temptation to control him and instead, offer him the trust and respect he needs – treat him as a leader and he will be at your beck and call. The simple, yet foundational equation of marriage is that men want respect and women want love. When a man gets respect, he gives love. When the wife gets love, she shows respect.

While mainstream society has reversed this dynamic, there are indeed many women who do wish to live like this, needing not to worry about the burden of financially providing. They do not want to be responsible or take charge, but instead focus on the needs of their homes, children, and husbands. However, we must admit that in many cases, women reject this role due to the sheer abuse of the man's leadership role that occurs. Such ignorant men see their authority as a power trip, humiliating their wives with financial manipulation until she comes to resent this financial dynamic, as she was well provided for before getting married in the first place. In these cases, it is important for men to appraise their own leadership skills and have the courage to accept that perhaps their wives are not rejecting the idea of wifeliness, but rejecting their husband's misunderstanding or misapplication of it.

Putting this principle into practice

1. Learn about honourable forms of effective leadership

Husbands, whether through the vast ocean of wisdom within the *sīrah* or contemporary books written on the essential ingredients of leadership, must make an active effort to learn about exactly what their role entails. The common misconception of leaders as solitary, uncompromising authorities over helpless subjects is a backwards, ineffective, and harmful perception. Those who have researched this area deeply always refer back to the same conclusions: effective leaders are in the service of others; they are open to listening to feedback; they remain humble and self-reflective, yet can act decisively when it matters. Upholding the role of a leader within your home, is one of the most important jobs you can have as a man – as this is the life and afterlife of your family, that is at stake. Take time to learn about how you may best fulfil this role.

2. Allow a healthy dynamic to be established within the home

My sisters, under the successful leadership of your husband, you are not inferior, infantilised, or degraded. The differing roles we are all given come with their rights and responsibilities, and we will all be accountable for how we behave with the authority we were given. Show your husband that you trust him, support him, and are there to make his life easier. Show him respect as a wife first and model this for your children, so they see their father as their first hero. Do not allow the acidic discourse around you to interfere with the natural roles both you and your husband have been given, and you will see how Allah's apportioning of roles leads to the strongest and happiest families. Support your husband in his role and you will see him flourish into being a leader you are proud to stand alongside.

CHAPTER TEN

On the beauty of gratitude

وَإِذْ تَأَذَّنَ رَبُّكُمْ لَئِن شَكَرْتُمْ لَأَزِيدَنَّكُمْ

And when your Lord proclaimed, "If you are grateful, I will surely increase you." [103]

It is difficult to overstate the power of gratitude when applied to any aspect of your life. The benefit of practicing gratitude is not only repeatedly reinforced to us through the foundational texts of the Qur'an and Sunnah, but is a universally recognised virtue that transcends all cultures, beliefs, and systems of living. Self-help industries are rife with content centred on "gratitude" and seek to offer the psychological and practical benefits of actively practicing this virtue.

Gratitude involves a metaphysical equation that applies universally in life: the presence of gratitude = an increase in things to be grateful for, whereas ingratitude = an increase in things to complain about. It is an unbreakable law as predictable as the daily rising of the sun and as immutable as the Newtonian physics. Gratitude only ever invites goodness into your life, as al-Biqāʿī ﷺ said:

[103] *Ibrāhīm*, 14:7.

الشُّكْرُ قَيْدُ المَوْجُودِ وَصَيْدُ المَفْقُودِ

Gratitude is the chain for what you possess, and the bait for what you do not.

Gratitude is a beloved characteristic to Allah ﷻ simply because it is the acknowledgement, recognition, and appreciation of what you've been given, not what you want more of.

However, like everything, the gulf between theory and practice can be regrettably stark. It seems to be a human tendency to take for granted, especially the things and people nearest to us. When you are newly married, everything your spouse does for you feels so special. As time goes by, your husband going out to work hard and earn for the family becomes normal, and in a few years' time, it becomes "his duty anyway". Similarly, at the beginning, every meal your new bride cooked was delightful, then, as the years wore on, somehow the salt is always too little or too much, until eventually she is "not doing me a favour just by doing her job."

What has happened here? The attention you paid to acts of care began to wither away with time. The thankfulness you expressed dimmed into an indifferent shoulder shrug and the goodness that you were once so appreciative of became "normal", expected, and routine. The roles both husband and wife play did not change; instead, the heart's response becomes numb and ungrateful. Gratitude is a lens, a way of seeing the world that does not necessarily depend on the material reality around you. It is a mindset of focusing on the good and amplifying it in your heart and soul. We often hear the cliché of those who are "poor but happy" in comparison to the "wealthy" who can feel no joy no matter how many properties, fast cars, or luxuries they enjoy. Though simplistic, these ideas are useful for driving home an important message: gratitude is a mindset. It is not about having more; it is about loving and being content with what you have.

Putting this principle into practice

Imam Ibn al-Qayyim ﷺ stated, speaking about gratitude to Allah ﷻ:

الشُّكْرُ يَكُونُ بِالقَلْبِ خُضُوعًا وَاسْتِكَانَةً وَباللِّسَانِ ثَنَاءً وَاعْتِرَافًا وَبِالجَوَارِحِ طَاعَةً وَانْقِيَادًا

Gratitude is expressed in the heart through humility and submission, in the tongue through praise and acknowledgement, and in the limbs through obedience and compliance.[104]

Here is how we can seamlessly apply the act of expressive gratitude to marriage.

1. Thank inwardly

This is to feel indebted first to Allah ﷻ and then to your spouse, who – out of all people – chose you to be their life partner. The deepest gratitude comes from the heart. It is not merely an intellectual or tick-box exercise, but a deeply contemplative practice.

The Prophet ﷺ said in connection to this:

لَيَلْقَيَنَّ أَحَدُكُمْ رَبَّهُ يَوْمَ القِيَامَةِ فَيَقُولُ لَهُ: أَلَمْ أُسَخِّرْ لَكَ الخَيْلَ وَالإِبِلَ؟ أَلَمْ أَذَرْكَ تَرْأَسُ وَتَرْبَعُ؟ أَلَمْ أُزَوِّجْكَ فُلَانَةَ خَطَبَهَا الخُطَّابُ فَمَنَعْتُهُمْ وَزَوَّجْتُكَ

One of you will meet his Lord on the Day of Judgement and He will say to him, "Did I not give you horses and camels? Did I not give you authority? Did I not marry you to so and so, although others had asked for her hand, but I kept them away and married her to you?"[105]

Similarly, the Prophet ﷺ expressed gratitude for his wife, Khadījah ﷺ:

[104] Ibn al-Qayyim, *Madārij al-Sālikīn.*

[105] Al-Bukhārī, *Ṣaḥīḥ al-Bukhārī;* Muslim, *Ṣaḥīḥ Muslim.*

قد آمَنَتْ بي إذ كفرَ بي الناسُ وصدَّقَتْني إذ كذَّبَني الناسُ وواسَتْني بمالِها إذ حرَمَني الناسُ ورزَقَني اللهُ عزَّ وجلَّ ولَدَها إذ حرَمَني أولادَ النِّساءِ

She had faith in me when others disbelieved; she believed me when others belied me; she comforted me with her wealth when others deprived me; and Allah blessed me with children through her and withheld them from other women.[106]

Brothers, when your wife is taking care of the children, stop to consider the endless hours of unseen labour required to meet all the physical, emotional, practical, and developmental needs of small humans. Consider how you can fulfil your commitments outside of the house because you have the peace of mind that the home environment is taken care of. The luxury of fresh meals cooked and clean clothes prepared for you should be a cause for deep gratitude for all the care at the forefront of those tasks.

Similarly, for women, it may be easy to disregard the fact that your husband leaves the house every day to work, graft, and provide an income to keep your household afloat. The unseen work of bills that are paid, groceries that are covered, and the endless financial expenditures of children being taken care of should be a source of gratitude. All of this is being done for you, so you do not have to fend for yourself or be ridden with anxiety over money and earning. This is something to actively remind yourself of in case the dynamic gets so normalised that both the roles of husband and wife are seen as mere duties being fulfilled, not acts of care for the interest of the family.

Does your spouse pray regularly? Praise Allah ﷻ for another thing to be genuinely grateful for.

[106] Ibn Ḥanbal, *Musnad Aḥmad.*

Does your spouse generally make himself/herself available to you? Praise Allah ﷻ and be grateful to Him and then her, remembering the days when you were alone with your desires and had no companion other than the whisperings of Shayṭān.

One of the most harmful ideas that threatens marital contentment is the illusion of the grass being greener on the other side. This is rarely the case, and points to a malignant ingratitude that must be remedied. When we look towards others, we only see their blessings and never their hardships. When we look at our own situations, wc tend to amplify the hardships and gloss over our blessings. The reality is that every person's life is a unique blend of challenges and blessings determined by Allah ﷻ, and that "over there" is never a place of perfection. Look at what you have, and you will begin to notice even more things to be grateful for. When you look at what you lack, then you risk launching yourself into a bottomless pit where nothing can, or ever will, satisfy you.

2. Express thanks verbally

How common it is in mediation sessions to hear one spouse say to another: "...but you know I love you honey!" Just think: if you are expected to express gratitude to Allah ﷻ verbally and He is the One who knows what is within your heart, what then of weak human beings who are incapable of reading your thoughts or the state of your heart? On this,

William Arthur Ward said, "Feeling gratitude and not expressing it is like wrapping a present and not giving it."

Regardless of how cheesy or difficult it may feel, we need to verbalise these feelings. Once, a man was with the Prophet ﷺ when another man passed in front of them, the man with the Prophet ﷺ said, "O Messenger of Allah! I love this man." The Messenger of Allah ﷺ then asked, "Have you informed him?"

He replied: "No." The Prophet ﷺ commanded him to do so, and thus he then went to the other man and said, "I love you for Allah's sake." He replied, "May He for Whose sake you love me love you!"[107]

If such was the advice of Prophet Muhammad ﷺ to two unrelated Companions, then surely our spouses are certainly even more deserving of hearing such words. The Prophet Muhammad ﷺ said:

مَنْ صُنِعَ إِلَيْهِ مَعْرُوفٌ فَقَالَ لِفَاعِلِهِ جَزَاكَ اللَّهُ خَيْرًا فَقَدْ أَبْلَغَ فِي الثَّنَاءِ

Whoever to whom some good was done, and he says "jazāk Allāhu khayran" (may Allah reward you with goodness), then he has done the most that he can of praise.[108]

Indeed it is painful – and sadly too common – when the words "thank you" and "jazākum Allåhu khayran" (may Allah reward you with goodness) is exclusively said to strangers, friends, and neighbours while ingratitude is the norm with the family members who deserve it the most.

Gratitude towards husbands is especially important, as the Prophet ﷺ said:

لَا يَنْظُرُ اللهُ إِلَى امْرَأَةٍ لَا تَشْكُرُ لِزَوْجِهَا وَهِيَ لَا تَسْتَغْنِي عَنْهُ

Allah does not look at a woman who does not show gratitude to her husband, despite her not being able to do without him.[109]

In another narration, the Prophet ﷺ said:

أُرِيتُ النَّارَ فَإِذَا أَكْثَرُ أَهْلِهَا النِّسَاءُ، يَكْفُرْنَ قِيلَ: أَيَكْفُرْنَ بِاللَّهِ؟ قَالَ: يَكْفُرْنَ الْعَشِيرَ وَيَكْفُرْنَ الإِحْسَانَ لَوْ أَحْسَنْتَ إِلَى إِحْدَاهُنَّ الدَّهْرَ ثُمَّ رَأَتْ مِنْكَ شَيْئًا قَالَتْ: مَا رَأَيْتُ مِنْكَ خَيْرًا قَطُّ

[107] Abū Dāwūd, *Sunan Abū Dāwūd*.
[108] Al-Tirmidhī, *Jāmiʿ al-Tirmidhī*.
[109] Al-Nasāʾī, *As-Sunan al-Ṣughrā li al-Nasāʾī*.

"I was shown Hell and I saw that the majority of its people are women." It was said, "Why, O Messenger of Allah?" He said, "Because of their ingratitude." It was said, "Are they ungrateful to Allah?" He said, "They are ungrateful to their companions (husbands) and ungrateful for good treatment. If you are kind to one of them for a lifetime, then she sees one (undesirable) thing in you, she will say, 'I have never seen anything good from you.'"[110]

3. Thank practically

The Prophet Muhammad ﷺ said:

مَنْ آتَى إِلَيْكُمْ مَعْرُوفًا فَكَافِئُوهُ فَإِنْ لَمْ تَجِدُوا فَادْعُوا اللَّهَ لَهُ حَتَّى تَعْلَمُوا أَنْ قَدْ كَافَأْتُمُوهُ

Whoever does you a favour, then reciprocate it, and if you cannot, then supplicate for him until you think that you have repaid him.[111]

If this advice refers to mere "favours", what then of a spouse who has devoted their life, ambitions, and future to you?

ways of showing your gratitude are assisting one another in practical ways, taking the load off each other, gifting each other generously, and of course, always remaining faithful to each other – the greatest manifestation of marital gratitude.

In fact, Makhlad ibn al-Ḥusayn ﵀ defined gratitude as being:

كَانَ يُقَالُ: الشُّكْرُ تَرْكُ الْمَعْصِيَةِ

It used to be said, "gratitude is abstinence from sin."[112]

[110] Al-Bukhārī, *Ṣaḥīḥ al-Bukhārī*.
[111] Abū Dāwūd, *Sunan Abū Dāwūd*.
[112] Ibn Abī al-Dunyā, *Kitāb al-Shukr*.

It is only when your eyes start to wander, your affectionate words begin to fall on the ears of those other than your spouse, and your attention becomes misplaced, that you start to see your relationship fall apart. Your wellbeing and sanity soon go along with it, as you realise just how ungrateful you had been firstly to Allah ﷻ who blessed you with a reasonable spouse, and secondly to the spouse whom you took for granted and stopped seeing the goodness in. The principle mentioned in the title has two parts: "And when your Lord proclaimed, 'If you are grateful, I will surely increase you, and if you are ungrateful, then My punishment is severe.'" Forget not the consequences of this second counterpart.

You will begin to experience firsthand the second part of this principle in the form of dysfunctional family, children who suffer trauma from the feeling that their father or mother traded them for other children, major financial changes due to a divorce settlement, broken trust that is very difficult to repair, a cancerous sore of guilt for such poor decisions in life, a crippling sense of shame, and vulnerability to every form of pain. At this point, you may even experience a brand-new appreciation for your spouse; however, by this point, it will be far too late for those realisations to be of any use to you. This will then compound the crippling guilt, which sits alongside the extreme anxiety of how to answer in the Hereafter for the harm your ingratitude caused.

Ibn Zurayq al-Baghdādī penned a saddening couplet of poetry, found next to him after he had passed away as an estranged traveler, having regretted not responding to the pleas of his wife to not travel:

رُزِقتُ مُلكاً فَلَم أَحسِن سِياسَتَهُ * وَكُلُّ مَن لا يُسُوسُ المُلكَ يَخلَعُهُ

وَمَن غَدا لابِساً ثَوبَ النَعِيم بِلا * شَكرٍ عَلَيهِ فَإِنَّ اللهَ يَنزَعُهُ

> I was blessed with a kingdom, but I did not govern it wisely, and every person who mishandles a kingdom will have it taken away. And whoever wears a garment of blessings without gratitude, then Allah will strip him of that garment.

In today's world, the pursuit of happiness and individual satisfaction has become a religion of its own, yet it is one, however, that enslaves mankind rather than freeing him. It shackles its believers, since the "religion" focuses on what you think you need, as opposed to what you have. Human rights come with human responsibilities. As younger generations sink deeper into this self-centric discourse, which places the individual at the centre of the universe, the possibility of contentment evaporates for those who prioritise their desires and the pursuit of an unattainable earthly utopia over gratitude.

It is not surprising, therefore, to see that Allah ﷻ no longer forms the basis for the choices people make in their worldly or spiritual goals. In the current era of 'me' has clearly produced a deep void and has crippled our capacity for gratitude. Reclaim yourself from this malaise by bringing clear order to your life. Allah's Pleasure is your foremost priority; your marriage is an excellent vehicle by which to arrive at that destination, and a strong and consistent practice of gratitude is the fuel that will drive you safely – together – to your destination.

CHAPTER ELEVEN

On overlooking with wisdom

عَرَّفَ بَعْضَهُ وَأَعْرَضَ عَنْ بَعْضٍ

He made known part of it and ignored a part.[113]

This verse from the Qur'an was revealed in response to a specific situation that arose between the Prophet ﷺ and some of his wives. Allah ﷻ highlights that when addressing the issue, the Prophet ﷺ focused on certain aspects of his wife's actions while overlooking others.

Failing to overlook faults and giving in to the urge to hone in on every shortcoming and mistake is a sure-fire way to wear down a relationship and erode any goodwill between you and your spouse. In fact, constant criticism was considered a major predictor of divorce according to the eminent relationship expert Professor John Gottman. Those who have experienced this know very well that it is torturous to be around someone who is constantly remarking about your flaws and blaming you for your shortcomings. Over time, being too critical in your relationship will whittle away at the healthy and joyful parts of the connection. Such criticism is expressed through disapprov-

[113] *Al-Taḥrīm*, 66:3.

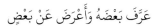

ing, critiquing, correcting, blaming, nit-picking, or seeking to "fix" your partner.

No human being is perfect or complete in every sense. "Deficiency" is a deeply-rooted characteristic of each and every one of us. After coming to grips with this reality, we should understand the importance of a very beautiful art and a noble characteristic which only a select few have mastered – this is the art of "taghāful".

What is taghāful? It could be vaguely defined as "to overlook", but a deeper explanation can be found in the following definition:

تَكَلُّفُ الغَفْلَةِ مَعَ العِلْمِ وَالإِدْرَاكِ لِمَا يُتَغَافَلُ عَنْهُ تَكَرُّمًا وَتَرَفُّعًا عَنْ سَفَاسِفِ الأُمُورِ

To purposefully ignore something whilst being fully aware of that which you are ignoring, but doing so out of nobility and rising above lowly, petty matters.[114]

This practice is a reflection of the words of our Prophet ﷺ, who said:

إِنَّ اللَّهَ يُحِبُّ مَعَالِيَ الأُمُورِ وَأَشْرَافَهَا وَيَكْرَهُ سَفْسَافَهَا

Allah loves the noblest and most honourable of matters and hates petty trivial matters.[115]

How many cherished relationships, whether with a spouse or others, have people lost because they remained fixated on their flaws and scrutinised every misstep? As you grow wiser and mature, you will learn the value of adopting a "let it go" mindset, which will allow you to move beyond trivial imperfections and focus on the bigger picture.

---

[114] Abū Shanār, *Faḍā'il al-Akhlāq fī Ḍaw' al-Kitāb wa al-Sunnah.*

[115] al-Ṭabarānī, *Muʿjam al-Kabīr li al-Ṭabarānī.*

In the days when our beloved Prophet Muhammad ﷺ walked the Earth, the Pagans of Mecca sought to diminish his noble name "Muhammad", which means "the praised one." They twisted the letters around and would maliciously utter "mud-hammam", which means "the reviled one." Yet, reflect on the profound response of our Prophet ﷺ in the face of such insults, when he said:

$$\text{أَلَا تَعْجَبُونَ كَيْفَ يَصْرِفُ اللَّهُ عَنِّي شَتْمَ قُرَيْشٍ وَلَعْنَهُمْ يَشْتِمُونَ مُذَمَّمًا وَيَلْعَنُونَ مُذَمَّمًا وَأَنَا مُحَمَّدٌ}$$

Do you not find it amazing how Allah repels their insults away from me? They are swearing at a person called mudhammam and cursing him, but I am Muhammad![116]

One might question, did our Prophet ﷺ not recognise that he is the very person the Quraysh were alluding to when cursing "mudhammam"? Undoubtedly, he did, but herein lies the brilliance of taghāful, the art of gracefully overlooking. He demonstrates to us the wisdom of not getting entangled in insignificant details, but rather fixing our gaze upon the weightier matters and therefore elevating ourselves to a higher plane of conduct.

In a previous chapter, we shared the narration of Umm Zarʿ, where ʿĀʾishah ؓ shared the story of eleven women who gathered and promised each other that they would speak about their husbands without notifying the Prophet ﷺ. As the story goes, some of them spoke highly of their spouses whilst others spoke critically. The description provided by the fifth woman about her husband directly relates to the subject of overlooking faults, saying:

---

[116] Al-Bukhārī, *Ṣaḥīḥ al-Bukhārī*.

زَوْجِي إِذَا دَخَلَ فَهِدَ وَإِذَا خَرَجَ أَسِدَ وَلَا يَسْأَلُ عَمَّا عَهِدَ

My husband behaves like a leopard when he enters the house and behaves like a lion when he goes out, and he does not ask about what he has entrusted.[117]

Explaining her description of her husband being "like a leopard", Ibn Baṭṭāl ﷺ said, "She is describing him as an excessive sleeper and commenting on how he overlooks matters within the house, as leopards are known to sleep a lot. She is implying that he overlooks the money of his that has been spent by her, and that he does not reproach her for any flaws of the house, as if oblivious to them."[118]

When Imam Aḥmad Ibn Ḥanbal ﷺ heard of a man, ʿUthmān ibn Zā'idah ﷺ, who said, "Well-being consists of ten parts, nine of which are in taghāful", Imam Aḥmad ﷺ said:

العَافِيَةُ عَشَرَةُ أَجْزَاءٍ تِسْعَةٌ مِنْهَا فِي التَّغَافُلِ

Well-being consists of ten parts, all of which are in taghāful.[119]

Just as you cannot completely meet all the expectations of your spouse, it is unrealistic to expect your spouse to always meet all your expectations. It is within this context that the true essence and beauty of practicing taghāful come to light. It is a manifest demonstration of wisdom, maturity and honour.

For this reason, al-Ḥasan al-Baṣrī ﷺ stated:

مَا اسْتَقْصَى كَرِيمٌ قَطُّ

An honourable person never investigates meticulously.[120]

---

[117] Al-Bukhārī, *Ṣaḥīḥ al-Bukhārī*

[118] Ibn Baṭṭāl, *Sharḥ Ṣaḥīḥ al-Bukhārī.*

[119] Al-Bayhaqī, *Shuʿab al-Īmān.*

[120] Al-Qurṭubī, *Tafsīr al-Qurṭubī.*

In other words, noble souls of high integrity tend to prioritise harmony, forgiveness, and generosity over being excessively critical or probing deeply into the failings of others, and refrain from prying into personal matters, avoiding unnecessary scrutiny or investigation into matters that do not concern them.

It is essential to emphasise that not every instance of offensive behaviour should be disregarded or overlooked. Wrongdoings involving the mistreatment of others or the violation of Allah's rights demand immediate and tactful intervention. The Prophet ﷺ said:

مَنْ رَأَى مِنْكُمْ مُنْكَرًا فَلْيُغَيِّرْهُ بِيَدِهِ، فَإِنْ لَمْ يَسْتَطِعْ فَبِلِسَانِهِ، فَإِنْ لَمْ يَسْتَطِعْ فَبِقَلْبِهِ، وَذَلِكَ أَضْعَفُ الْإِيمَانِ

> Whoever among you sees an evil, let him change it with his hand. If he is unable to do so, then with his tongue, and if he is unable to do so, then with his heart, and that is the weakest level of faith.[121]

Relatively, the Qur'anic principle "He made known part of it and ignored a part" urges us to turn a blind eye when our spouses lapse within reason. Sparing the harsh commentary today will often reap dividends tomorrow when the issue has blown over, and from choosing to do so, your goodwill with one another will remain intact. Regular nitpicking risks inflaming an issue and – on top of the initial "fault" you were criticising – putting you in a position where you are now being resented for being so negative and judgemental. Such behaviour quickly depletes the affection and love between two people, so always opt for the higher virtue in the appropriate matters.

---

[121] Muslim, *Ṣaḥīḥ Muslim*.

Putting this principle into practice

1. Understand where your habit of nitpicking came from

Do you search for the fault in others because your own faults were constantly called out during your own childhood? Is the constant criticism you received from your parents now echoing through your own voice in adulthood? Do you nitpick as a misguided cry for attention, somehow feeling that any attention is better than no attention? Is your nitpicking masking a deeper resentment that has been building up and is now resurfacing. Could your nitpicking simply be because you have too much free time on your hands, or because you are just a generally negative person? Each of these questions should be considered and addressed accordingly, with the relevant actions taken to resolve these issues. We are all adults that need to be accountable to ourselves for the way we behave. Perhaps you may not be to blame for the behaviours of your upbringing, but you certainly have the responsibility to recognise this and remedy it now before the harm seeps into another generation.

2. Pause and comprehend what you are about to say

Are you focused on the rose or the thorn? If the thorn, how important is your comment in the grand scheme of things? Unless the house is on fire and someone's shutting off the water, rethink your words, or practice keeping them to yourself. What might seem a reasonable offhand comment to you may leave lasting injury to your spouse, and words can never be unspoken.

3. Use the "sandwich approach" or "hamburger method"

This approach is touted as a valuable technique for tackling challenging conversations by many business leaders. The "sandwich approach" is when a manager offers a piece of negative feedback "sandwiched" between two positive ones, thus easing the blow of the critique. Keep your criticisms for the important things, since too much negative "feedback" will desensitise people to anything you have to say. When you do judge the issue to be important enough to bring up, then:

- Speak clearly and to the point, without bringing up past issues or behaviours.
- Keep the shortcoming within perspective and cushion your language with words like, "This isn't a really big deal, but I just wanted to mention…"
- Reaffirm your intentions in bringing up the topic, and reassure your spouse of your care, affection, and appreciation for them.

You are obviously going to have confrontations when you are in a long-term relationship with someone, but you do not have to have them constantly. Decide which issues are worth confronting and which are not. At times you will need to turn a blind eye to something that irritates you and concede to lose a battle to win the war.

All long-term relationships have issues involving personality traits or temperamental qualities, and these risk causing perpetual conflict. These unsolvable problems are things you simply need to learn to live with. Learn to pick your battles and save your arguments for the big issues. When you keep expressing irritation towards the habits of your spouse and trying to reform their behaviour, you often cause them to resent "your help" so much that they may even rebel against you. In any case, nit-picking is a lowly move of poor social and emotional intelligence and a significant way to demolish your appeal and attractiveness as a wife or charisma and leadership as a husband. Your marriage is far too important to ever allow this to occur. Focus on your spouse's goodness, and handle their shortcomings with care, wisdom, and foresight.

CHAPTER TWELVE

On reconciling with sincerity

وَالصُّلْحُ خَيْرٌ

And reconciliation is best.[122]

Human interactions, whether with a spouse, family, friends, or colleagues, are inherently complex. Expecting to have seamless experiences with others is an unrealistic expectation, as conflicting interests, misunderstandings, and mistreatment are unfortunately common aspects of relationships. What distinguishes successful relationships from broken or dysfunctional ones is the presence of a crucial element: the sincere act of reconciliation. Without it, each of us would simply accrue a string of broken relationships every time we ran into difficult times with each other. It is for this reason that Islam showers praise upon reconciliation as a religious priority:

Allah ﷻ said:

لَا خَيْرَ فِي كَثِيرٍ مِنْ نَجْوَاهُمْ إِلَّا مَنْ أَمَرَ بِصَدَقَةٍ أَوْ مَعْرُوفٍ أَوْ إِصْلَاحٍ بَيْنَ النَّاسِ وَمَنْ يَفْعَلْ ذَلِكَ ابْتِغَاءَ مَرْضَاتِ اللَّهِ فَسَوْفَ نُؤْتِيهِ أَجْرًا عَظِيمًا

[122] *Al-Nisā'*, 4:128.

There is no good in most of their secret conversations except those who enjoin charity or goodness or reconciliation between people; and whoever does this seeking Allah's pleasure, We will give him a mighty reward.[123]

In the case of two warring camps of Muslims, Allah ﷻ says:

فَإِنْ بَغَتْ إِحْدَاهُمَا عَلَى الْأُخْرَى فَقَاتِلُوا الَّتِي تَبْغِي حَتَّى تَفِيءَ إِلَى أَمْرِ اللَّهِ فَإِنْ فَاءَتْ فَأَصْلِحُوا بَيْنَهُمَا بِالْعَدْلِ وَأَقْسِطُوا إِنَّ اللَّهَ يُحِبُّ الْمُقْسِطِينَ

If one of them transgresses against the other, fight against the transgressing group until they submit to the rule of Allah. Then if they submit, make peace between them with fairness, and be just, for Allah loves those who are just.[124]

Furthermore, when the Companions ﷺ once disputed with each other about how the spoils of war ought to be distributed, Allah ﷻ revealed the initial verses from Sūrah al-Anfāl that ostensibly appeared to have very little to do with their question:

يَسْأَلُونَكَ عَنِ الْأَنْفَالِ قُلِ الْأَنْفَالُ لِلَّهِ وَالرَّسُولِ فَاتَّقُوا اللَّهَ وَأَصْلِحُوا ذَاتَ بَيْنِكُمْ وَأَطِيعُوا اللَّهَ وَرَسُولَهُ إِنْ كُنْتُمْ مُؤْمِنِينَ

They ask you concerning the spoils of war? Tell them: "The spoils of war belong to Allah and the Messenger. So fear Allah, and set things right between you, and obey Allah and His Messenger if you are true believers."[125]

The question regarding the division of spoils was not immediately answered in detail, only being given further explanation forty verses later. This deliberate delay carries a significant lesson from Allah ﷻ to the Companions ﷺ as well as to all believers: it emphasises that fostering unity within the community holds far greater importance than the distribution of worldly possessions.

---

123 *Al-Nisā'*, 4:114.
124 *Al-Ḥujarāt*, 49:9.
125 *Al-Anfāl*, 8:1.

Similarly, in the context of marriage, Allah ﷻ encourages couples to make peace between themselves, wherever possible, and says, *"And reconciliation is best."* [126]

Allah ﷻ said:

وَإِنِ امْرَأَةٌ خَافَتْ مِن بَعْلِهَا نُشُوزًا أَوْ إِعْرَاضًا فَلَا جُنَاحَ عَلَيْهِمَا أَن يُصْلِحَا بَيْنَهُمَا صُلْحًا وَالصُّلْحُ خَيْرٌ

And if a woman fears disobedience or turning away from her husband, then there is no blame on them if they make peace between themselves, and peace is better.[127]

In the process of making peace or achieving reconciliation, it is often necessary for one or both parties involved to make sacrifices or relinquish certain rights to prevent the complete breakdown of their relationship. This can involve compromises in various aspects of marital life, such as lifestyle, spending habits, standard of living, or even the amount of time spent together. It is crucial for couples to approach their relationship in a holistic manner, such that minor issues are evaluated in the context of the bigger picture. Insisting on an inflexible stance regarding trivial matters can ultimately jeopardise the overall well-being of the marriage. Therefore, it is important to prioritise the greater good of the relationship and be willing to make smaller concessions to preserve the harmony and longevity of the relationship.

The Prophet's ﷺ endeavours to keep marriages intact.

The Prophet Muhammad ﷺ inspired the believers to broaden their perspectives and think beyond their immediate circumstances. He wisely advised them to consider the bigger picture, encouraging a macro-level outlook, saying:

---

[126] *Al-Nisā'*, 4:128.
[127] *Al-Nisā'*, 4:128.

لَا يَفْرَكْ مُؤْمِنٌ مُؤْمِنَةً إِنْ سَخِطَ مِنْهَا خُلُقًا رَضِيَ مِنْهَا آخَرَ

A believing man (husband) must not despise a believing woman (wife). If he hates one of her traits, then he is surely pleased with another.[128]

Commenting on this Hadith, al-Qāḍī ʿIyāḍ ﷺ said:

وَفِيهِ إِشَارَةٌ إِلَى أَنَّ الصَّاحِبَ لَا يُوجَدُ بِدُونِ عَيْبٍ، فَإِنْ أَرَادَ الشَّخْصُ بَرِيئًا مِنَ الْعَيْبِ يَبْقَى بِلَا صَاحِبٍ، وَلَا يَخْلُو الْإِنْسَانُ سِيَّمَا الْمُؤْمِنُ عَنْ بَعْضِ خِصَالٍ حَمِيدَةٍ، فَيَنْبَغِي أَنْ يُرَاعِيَهَا وَيَسْتُرَ مَا بَقِيَ

This Hadith indicates that no companion is free from faults. If, however, one aspires for another who is fault-free, he will remain without a friend. No human being, particularly the believer, is without some virtuous traits, which one should acknowledge and conceal the rest.[129]

There was a companion named Mughīth ﷺ who was married to a woman named Barīrah ﷺ. However, Barīrah ﷺ had lost interest in her husband. ʿAbdullāh ibn ʿAbbās ﷺ said:

كَأَنِّي أَنْظُرُ إِلَيْهِ يَطُوفُ خَلْفَهَا يَبْكِي ودُمُوعُهُ تَسِيلُ علَى لِحْيَتِهِ

I remember vividly how he used to walk behind her in the streets with tears streaming off his beard.

The Prophet ﷺ said to Ibn ʿAbbās ﷺ:

يا عَبَّاسُ أَلَا تَعْجَبُ مِن حُبِّ مُغِيثٍ بَرِيرَةَ ومِنْ بُغْضِ بَرِيرَةَ مُغِيثًا!

O ʿAbbās, are you not amazed at the love Mughīth has for Barīrah, and the hatred Barīrah has for Mughīth?

The Prophet attempted to reconcile between them, saying to Barīrah, "Would you reconsider him, for he is the father of your child." She said, "O Messenger of Allah, do you command

[128] Muslim, *Ṣaḥīḥ Muslim*.
[129] ʿAlī al-Qārī, *Mirqāh al-Mafātīḥ*.

me?" He replied, "I only intercede." She said, "I have no need for him."[130]

In a similar narration, the Prophet ﷺ once visited the home of his daughter, Fāṭimah , but her husband was not home. He asked, "Where is your cousin (ʿAlī)?", to which she responded:

كَانَ بَيْنِي وَبَيْنَهُ شَيْءٌ فَغَاضَبَنِي فَخَرَجَ فَلَمْ يَقِلْ عِنْدِي

We fell out over a matter, and so he left the house and chose not to take his siesta nap here.

The Prophet ﷺ inquired about his whereabouts and heard that he was in the masjid. The Prophet ﷺ then went to the masjid and found ʿAlī lying on the ground, fast asleep. Part of his body was uncovered and had become covered with dust from the earth beneath him. The Prophet ﷺ started patting the dust away from his body as he said to him affectionately:

قُمْ أَبَا تُرَابٍ قُمْ أَبَا تُرَابٍ

Get up O dusty one, get up O dusty one![131]

Several beneficial lessons can be gleaned from this remarkable incident:

1. The Prophet ﷺ asked his daughter "Where is your cousin?" (or literally, "Where is the son of your uncle?") as opposed to saying "Where is ʿAlī ?", so as to remind her that it is not just marriage that bonds them but family ties too. This is how responsible parents act, playing an active and mature role in rekindling harmony between their children.

---

[130] Al-Bukhārī, *Ṣaḥīḥ al-Bukhārī*.
[131] Al-Bukhārī, *Ṣaḥīḥ al-Bukhārī*.

2. Fāṭimah's ﷺ response to the query about the whereabouts of her husband displayed remarkable wisdom and maturity. Instead of delving into the specifics of the disagreement, expressing her side of the story in the absence of her husband, or seeking validation or sympathy, she chose to maintain privacy and dignity in the midst of their disagreement and simply stated, "We fell out over a matter." Her concise response demonstrated not only a level of restraint, respect for their relationship and emotional intelligence, but also contributed to the eventual resolution of the matter.

3. Rather than immediately summoning ʿAlī ﷺ or taking sides, the Prophet ﷺ actively sought out his whereabouts, demonstrating his concern for ʿAlī's well-being and avoiding any potential feelings of isolation or favouritism by instead humbly making his way towards him.

4. The Prophet Muhammad ﷺ displayed his comforting sense of humour and affectionate nature when addressing ʿAlī ﷺ when he found him sleeping in the masjid. With a light-hearted tone, the Prophet ﷺ called out to him, saying, "Get up, O dusty one!"

Indeed the way we respond to other people's problems can significantly influence their perception of those problems. When those around us magnify and exaggerate issues, they tend to loom larger in our own eyes, causing unnecessary strife and division. Instead, by using such endearing words, the Prophet ﷺ created an atmosphere of warmth and familiarity, immediately easing any potential tension or apprehension that ʿAlī ﷺ may have felt. This simple and light-hearted remark demonstrated the Prophet's ability to approach sensitive situations with kindness and playfulness, defusing any heavy or negative emotions that may have arisen.

Moreover, the Prophet's decision to send ʿAlī رضي الله عنه back home without delving into the details of his fallout with Fāṭimah demonstrated his trust in ʿAlī's integrity and the close bond they shared.

5. Fāṭimah رضي الله عنها did not complain to her father, nor did ʿAlī رضي الله عنه complain to the Prophet ﷺ, his father-in-law. This confidentiality, of course, is a priority for married couples to uphold wherever possible: to contain the issue as much as possible. When you bring in arbitrators, whether they are parents, friends, or trusted figures from the community, your priority should be to try and resolve the problem without making your issues public. There are many noble husbands and wives who fall into serious disputes with their spouses, yet the matter does not go beyond the walls of their homes, such that even the children are unaware of disputes between their parents. These are your personal family matters and should only be disclosed out of absolute necessity. Protect your household and do not allow your relationship to become the subject of other people's chit-chat.

The Companions' efforts to keep families together

The Companions رضي الله عنهم exemplified the spirit of reconciliation and made great efforts to repair marital relationships.

Once Asmāʾ رضي الله عنها, daughter of Abū Bakr رضي الله عنه and wife of al-Zubayr ibn al-ʿAwwām رضي الله عنه, felt troubled that her husband was strict with her. Feeling overwhelmed, she sought solace and support from her father, expressing her concerns about her husband's behaviour. Abū Bakr رضي الله عنه, in response, provided his daughter with gentle guidance and profound wisdom.

يَا بُنَيَّةُ اصْبِرِي فَإِنَّ الْمَرْأَةَ إِذَا كَانَ لَهَا زَوْجٌ صَالِحٌ ثُمَّ مَاتَ عَنْهَا فَلَمْ تَزَوَّجْ بَعْدَهُ جُمِعَ بَيْنَهُمَا فِي الْجَنَّةِ

O my daughter, be patient, for when a woman has a righteous husband and he passes away, and she does not remarry thereafter, they will be reunited in Paradise.[132]

This insightful advice from Abū Bakr ﵁ reflects his deep understanding of the complexities of marriage and the need for a broader perspective. This incident highlights the significant role that in-laws can play in supporting and reconciling couples.

Once, a man came to ʿUmar ibn al-Khaṭṭāb ﵁ to complain about the character of his wife, he stood at ʿUmar's door, waiting for him. While there, he overheard ʿUmar's wife berating ʿUmar ﵁, while ʿUmar ﵁ remained silent without responding. The man then left, saying, "If this is the state of the leader of the believers, ʿUmar ibn al-Khaṭṭāb, then what about my own situation?"

ʿUmar ﵁ came out and saw him leaving in distress, so he called out to him, "What is your need, my brother?" The man replied, "O leader of the believers, I had come to complain to you about the character of my wife and her disrespect towards me. I heard your wife doing the same, so I went back and said, 'If this is the state of the leader of the believers with his wife, then what about my own situation?'" ʿUmar ﵁ said to him:

إِنَّمَا تَحَمَّلْتُهَا لِحُقُوقٍ لَهَا عَلَيَّ: إِنَّهَا طَبَّاخَةٌ لِطَعَامِي خَبَّازَةٌ لِخُبْزِي غَسَّالَةٌ لِثِيَابِي رَضَّاعَةٌ لِوَلَدِي وَلَيْسَ ذَلِكَ بِوَاجِبٍ عَلَيْهَا وَيَسْكُنُ قَلْبِي بِهَا عَنِ الْحَرَامِ، فَأَنَا أَتَحَمَّلُهَا لِذَلِكَ

I only endure her for the rights she has over me: she cooks my food, bakes my bread, washes my clothes, nurses my children, and she is not obligated to do any of that. She also keeps my heart away from the unlawful. So I bear with her for these reasons.

---

[132] Ibn Saʿd, *al-Ṭabaqāt al-Kabīr*.

The man then continued, saying "O leader of the believers, my wife does these things too", upon which ʿUmar ﵁ replied:

فَتَحَمَّلْهَا يَا أَخِي فَإِنَّمَا هِيَ مُدَّةٌ يَسِيرَةٌ

So endure her my brother, for it is only a short period.[133]

The conversation between ʿUmar h and the man seeking advice about his wife's behaviour showcases the Companions' approach to resolving marital issues, in which they encouraged one another to prioritise understanding, patience, and the recognition of the rights and contributions of their spouses.

Steps towards reconciliation

The initial steps towards reconciliation can only be taken when you strive to maintain the appropriate scale and confidentiality of the dispute and its resolution. This involves the following:

1. Control your anger

Abū Hurayrah ﵁ narrates, "A man came to the Prophet ﷺ and said, 'Advise me.' The Prophet ﷺ said, 'Do not be angry.' The man repeated his request and the Prophet said, 'Do not be angry.'[134]

Speech strategies for anger management shall be discussed at length in the coming chapters.

---

[133] Al-Dhahabī, *al-Kabā'ir.*

[134] Al-Bukhārī, *Ṣaḥīḥ al-Bukhārī.*

2. Silence when angry

The Prophet ﷺ said:

إِذَا غَضِبَ أَحَدُكُمْ فَلْيَسْكُتْ

If one of you gets angry, let him be silent.[135]

Shaykh ʿAlī al-Ṭanṭāwī ﵀ once said:

I worked as a judge for twenty-seven years, and I found that most incidents of divorce are caused by the blind anger of a man and a woman's foolish response to that anger, despite the cause of the dispute being trivial!

3. When speaking, do not use accusatory language

Do not say "you did this", because as soon as you do so, you have triggered the defence mechanisms of your spouse and caused them to put up walls rather than channels of communication. Instead, use language that describes your feelings and subjective experience in the first person – "I felt hurt when this happened…" This way, instead of coming across as accusatory or hostile, you are explaining and expanding your own point of view.

4. Make concessions

If you are willing to accept "losing" an argument in order to save the marriage, then you will be truly successful. The opposite is also true – when the pride of the ego and Shayṭān's whisperings inflame an argument beyond all proportion, your entire marriage ends up becoming collateral for your stubbornness.

---

[135] Ibn Ḥanbal, *Musnad Aḥmad*.

Further stages towards reconciliation

If your problems really need a second opinion, then get others involved, as Allah ﷻ said:

وَإِنْ خِفْتُمْ شِقَاقَ بَيْنِهِمَا فَابْعَثُوا حَكَمًا مِنْ أَهْلِهِ وَحَكَمًا مِنْ أَهْلِهَا إِنْ يُرِيدَا إِصْلَاحًا يُوَفِّقِ اللَّهُ بَيْنَهُمَا

And if you fear dissension between the two, send an arbitrator from his family and an arbitrator from her family. If they both desire reconciliation, Allah will cause it between them.[136]

Many times, a problem can easily be resolved, but we need to hear this from someone else because our egos prevent us from accepting that same advice from our spouse.

The arbitrators entrusted with resolving marital disputes do not necessarily require PhD-level knowledge in Shariah, but rather they should possess wisdom and prioritise the well-being of your family. Their wisdom should enable them to recognise that the tears of a woman and the anger of a man do not, in isolation, serve as evidence of being right or wrong. They should also possess the skill to effectively manage a heated conversation without becoming entangled during emotional exchanges.

Whatever you do, do not let your marital life become the subject of chit-chat between yourself and friends. We can only wonder at how many marriages may have been saved, but failed purely as a result of bad marital advice from "friends" and parties who do not have the couple's best interests in mind. Do not hand over the keys to your relationship to those who are not worthy to hold them.

The opinions of such "friends" can be compared to the boisterous shouting of fans watching a sports match from the stands.

[136] *Al-Nisā'*, 4:35.

The fans can remove themselves from the game whenever they choose to do so, perhaps enjoying a hot dog, or may just leave the stadium if the game is boring. They are invested as long as the game is entertaining or interesting enough to hold their attention. The player, however, is on the field until the game is over, and such is the case for you and your spouse – you alone suffer the heartache of divorce should the marriage falter. The breakdown of your marriage is not something you can step away from with ease. The advice of such people is therefore useless in the best case, while in the worst case it is actively harmful.

Though it can be very comforting when friends and family gather on your side and declare war on your spouse or ex-spouse, this has minimal positive outcomes for anyone (including yourself). Those who cheerlead the end of a marriage rarely see the full picture of the marriage, are ignorant of many important facts, have only heard one side of the story, and may be completely ignorant of the Shariah and how to manage marital discord. For the health of your household and your children's futures, guard your marriage by only bringing such matters to those who are wise, skilled, and knowledgeable about them.

Conclusion

Marriage is the gold standard of commitment. It enables society to flourish by creating the most stable environment for family life and entails countless benefits for physical and mental health. However, marriages can and do break down. Considering this, couples should be encouraged to stay together and avoid divorce whenever possible, yet much of societal discourse pushes the narrative in the opposite direction, nearly glorifying divorce as an expression of individual will.

For example, in April 2022, "no-fault" divorces became legal in England and Wales. Under new legislation brought forward by the Conservative government in 2020, a person will be able to simply walk away from their marriage with no reason given, enabling unilateral divorce on demand. There is nothing the other party can do about it, even if that party has been grievously wronged by this decision or wants the marriage to continue.

Do not allow poor responses during a marital crises to cause you to lose out on character-building opportunities. Marital struggles are opportunities to grow, mature, and realise your own weaknesses. Taking the easy exit means running away from your problems rather than facing them or dealing with them immediately. If you do not unpack your issues and deal with them appropriately, then you will simply carry your negative traits (and even trauma) from one relationship to another, and more likely than not, history will repeat itself and you will land in the same difficulties in the future.

This does not mean every difficulty in a marriage is solvable, but neither does it mean that every source of tension is grounds for divorce. We deprive our children of a basic life skill when we say that the solution to every problem – or even just to boredom – is to walk away from it.

The most optimistic aspect of marriage is in the power of reconciliation. If both parties genuinely want to make the relationship work, and are willing to sincerely invest in their connection, then Allah ﷻ has promised to find a solution for them, and the promise of Allah ﷻ is never broken.

Putting this principle into action

1. Learn about your conflict style and that of your spouse

Every human is complex and unique, and is shaped by the particular circumstances of their upbringing, disposition and even genetic inheritance. All these aspects correlate to how people behave when faced with tension or conflict.

There are five general conflict styles: competing, collaborating, avoiding, accommodating, and compromising. These styles are based on where we are on a continuum between assertiveness and cooperation. In order to understand yourself and your spouse better, it is important to examine your reactions and seek to understand the underlying causes of those reactions. Ironically, and overwhelmingly, marriage researchers label conflict as something neutral, such that the only thing that makes it constructive or destructive is how we choose to respond to it. A healthy marriage is not about living forever without conflict, but rather being able to struggle well together.

2. Learn how *not* to communicate

In the heat of the moment, it is easy to blurt out the most hurtful and impulsive words that come to your mind. You may not even mean it, but once the words have escaped your lips, you set off a spiral of unpleasant and fruitless exchanges.

Professor John Gottman presented the most common maladaptive communication styles found in relationships, which are commonly referred to as the Four Horsemen of relationship dissatisfaction.

Consider the following categories, and while you read, ask yourself earnestly whether you fall into these patterns and consider how you can remain more cognisant of how you speak to your spouse and the consequences of your words on the health of your relationship:

1. **Criticisms**: these are explicit offensive statements or verbal attacks (e.g., "You just sit around all day while I'm at work.").
2. **Defensiveness**: this is a self-protective response to criticism that is often phrased as a counterattack (e.g., "I would not have forgotten to take the food in if you had cleaned out the refrigerator like I had asked you to do.").
3. **Contempt**: this involves deliberately causing emotional pain to someone else, and is rooted in feelings of disgust and disrespect for another person.
4. **Stonewalling**: this occurs when someone is unresponsive and withdraws from conversations rather than engaging in them.

The sad thing about each of these "horsemen" is that they often overlap and compound the feeling of negativity as a result: someone who feels contempt for their partner may criticise them, which may lead to their partner being defensive, which can then increase feelings of contempt. Additionally, stonewalling could compound feelings of contempt or further criticisms.

Once you commit yourself to trying to avoid these modes of communication, you must replace them with more productive and positive ways of saying the same thing. For example, rather than attacking a partner's general personality or image, rephrase complaints as specific needs that you have that may be unfulfilled. If you are feeling overwhelmed and not ready to engage in a certain conversation, explain this to your partner rather than storming out without an explanation. With time, care, and sincere effort, you will be able to express how you feel honestly while preserving the trust and goodwill of your spouse.

CHAPTER THIRTEEN

On seeking relief in Allah

وَمَنْ يَتَّقِ اللَّهَ يَجْعَلْ لَهُ مِنْ أَمْرِهِ يُسْرًا

And whoever fears Allah (or "has taqwā of Allah") – He will make his matters easy for him.[137]

These divine words carry a profound truth that breathes life into troubled marriages. Despite its brevity, there is a profound reassurance contained within this verse that, by embracing a conscious awareness of Allah's presence in our lives, we invite ease and serenity into our marriage, knowing that "He will make his matters easy for him."

Genuine fear of Allah ﷻ, far from instilling terror, awakens a reverence that transcends the temporal challenges of a relationship. It ignites a light within the souls of both partners, allowing them to rise above their own egos, such that, by virtue of their desire to glorify Allah ﷻ at every turn of their relationship, difficulties that once seemed insurmountable begin to melt away.

Taqwā is commonly associated with its visible manifestations, such as performing the five daily prayers, fasting, and avoiding the major sins of lying, alcohol consumption, and usury,

[137] *Al-Ṭalāq*, 65:4.

since taqwā is, at its core, the idea of shielding oneself from Allah's Wrath. However, the application of taqwā in the realm of marriage often goes unnoticed or is overlooked due to its subtle nature. Therefore, it is essential to explore how this can be practically applied within the context of marriage. Below are a few examples:

1. Fleeing to ṣalāh at the moment of marital distress

Hudhayfah ibn al-Yamān ﷺ said:

كان رسولُ اللهِ صلَّى اللهُ علَيهِ وسلَّمَ إذا حزَبه أمرٌ صلَّى

When a matter troubled the Messenger of Allah ﷺ, he would pray.[138]

It is imperative for both husband and wife to introspect and ponder over how often, since the inception of their marriage, have they sought refuge in ṣalāh when confronted with formidable hurdles in their marital journey? How frequently have they beseeched Allah ﷻ, through a devoted two-rakʿah prayer, imploring their Lord to aid them, manifest their aspirations, and bestow contentment upon their lives?

I know of an individual who was beset by domestic turmoil. Both his wife and children had become a source of immense anguish for him. When questioned about his course of action, he gestured towards a prayer rug nestled within the room, emphatically stating, "This!" He would hurriedly turn to it, praying to Allah ﷻ, seeking forgiveness, and imploring Him for help. Subsequently, Allah ﷻ, in His infinite mercy, orchestrated a transformative turn of events, whereby the happiness and clarity that had evaded him for years was finally restored to his household. How true is the promise of Allah ﷻ – "And whoever fears Allah (or 'has taqwā of Allah') – He will make his matters easy for him."

[138] Abū Dāwūd, *Sunan Abū Dāwūd.*

2. Prioritising your complaint to Allah

When a woman by the name of Khawlah bint Thaʿlabah ﵂ came to the Prophet ﷺ to complain about her husband, Aws ibn al-Ṣāmit ﵁, Allah ﷿ revealed verses in her regard, saying:

قَدْ سَمِعَ اللَّهُ قَوْلَ الَّتِي تُجَادِلُكَ فِي زَوْجِهَا وَتَشْتَكِي إِلَى اللَّهِ وَاللَّهُ يَسْمَعُ
تَحَاوُرَكُمَا إِنَّ اللَّهَ سَمِيعٌ بَصِيرٌ

Indeed, Allah has heard the argument of the woman who pleaded with you [O Prophet] concerning her husband, and appealed to Allah, and Allah has heard your exchange. Surely Allah is All-Hearing, All-Seeing.[139]

Khawlah ﵂ went to the Prophet ﷺ, taking the necessary human means after pouring out her complaint to her Lord beforehand. It was for this reason that relief came to her by way of revelation – Allah ﷿ lifted what burdened her and, as a testament to the far-reaching impact of her plea, Allah ﷿, in His infinite Wisdom, revealed rulings that not only brought relief to Khawlah ﵂, but also became a source of comfort and guidance for countless other women in similar situations. Truly, "whoever fears Allah (or 'has taqwā of Allah') – He will make his matters easy for him."

3. Refraining from invoking past favours to one another

In Arabic, such behaviour is referred to as al-mann, a toxic habit that erodes the foundation of any relationship, particularly marriage, tarnishing its purity and sincerity, and breeding resentment.

However, it is important to distinguish between the occasional need to remind someone of acts of kindness in a heated argument and the insidious act of leveraging past favours to demean and manipulate others.

[139] *Al-Mujādilah*, 58:1.

The Prophet ﷺ declared:

لَا يَدْخُلُ الجَنَّةَ مَنَّانٌ وَلَا عَاقٌّ وَلَا مُدْمِنُ خَمْرٍ

The "mannān" (one who reminds people of his favours), one who ill-treats their parents, and one addicted to alcohol will not enter Paradise.[140]

According to al-Qurṭubī ؒ, this attribute is often manifested in individuals who are both miserly and conceited. A miserly person tends to perceive their contributions as significant, even if they are trivial. On the other hand, a conceited person tends to elevate themselves, believing that they are bestowing great favours upon others through their giving. These attitudes stem from ignorance and a lack of remembrance regarding the blessings bestowed upon them by Allah ﷻ. If these individuals were to reflect deeply on life, they would realise that it is the recipient who is favouring them by providing an opportunity to earn rewards through their acts of giving.

4. Lowering the gaze

A person who upholds taqwā will see this attitude manifested in the purity of their gaze. A 2020 study published in the Journal of Sex Research found that 91.5% of men and 60.2% of women reported having used pornography within the previous month. Divorce lawyers have noticed a trend – porn is ruining marriage.

In a survey in 2002, the American Academy of Matrimonial Lawyers interviewed 350 divorce attorneys and found that roughly 60 percent reported that internet porn played a significant role in divorces. The same can be said regarding those who have opened up the window of obscenity into their lives in the form of social media feeds, such that the average child will see

[140] Al-Nasā'ī, *As-Sunan al-Ṣughrā li al-Nasā'ī*.

in one day what our grandparents may never have even seen in a lifetime. The rule is very clear: anybody who gets themselves addicted to fantasies will find their reality will suffer as a result.

Divorce lawyer James Sexton was asked in an interview why he labelled Facebook an "infidelity-generating machine". He replied:

"It is a huge factor now, and it is getting worse every day. I can't remember the last time I had a case where social media was not either a root cause or implicated in some way. And it is always the same story, starting with people maintaining affairs via social media or communicating with people they do not have any business communicating with. Infidelity is so easy in our times, and this is undoubtedly poisoning marriages.

The problem I have with Facebook specifically is that Facebook creates reasons of plausible deniability for you to be connecting with people emotionally in ways that are toxic to marriages. People use social media inappropriately when they're bored, vulnerable, or in transition – not when they're having a wonderful time with their spouse or enjoying life."

5. Making peace with Allah ﷻ following sin

Many individuals hold the misguided belief that as long as their personal sins do not directly harm others, they are acceptable and without consequences. They argue, "I'm not hurting anyone, so why should it matter?" However, this perspective could not be further from the truth, for it overlooks the profound impact of sin on the most vital entity in your life: your very soul. Sins carry repercussions that extend beyond the individual, affecting their relationship with Allah ﷻ and with fellow human beings. Conversely, the same principle applies to acts of piety and virtuous deeds.

Within the miracle of existence, we are all interconnected, and our actions invariably enact a ripple effect on one another. This timeless wisdom was eloquently expressed by John Donne, the seventeenth-century Dean of St. Paul's Cathedral, who proclaimed, "No man is an island, entire of itself; every man is a piece of the continent, a part of the main." Private decisions impact public life, and individual affairs shape our collective condition.

The Prophet ﷺ said:

مَا تَوَادَّ اثْنَانِ فِي اللهِ فَيُفَرَّقُ بَيْنَهُمَا إِلَّا بِذَنْبٍ يُحْدِثُهُ أَحَدُهُمَا

No two individuals who loved each other for the sake of Allah ended up separating except due to a sin committed by one of them.[141]

Can relationships withstand the divine consequences of unrepented sins? There is a plethora of verses in the Holy Qur'an and Prophetic Hadiths that speak about the impact of sins on the wellbeing of social order.

The great scholar Sufyān ibn ʿUyaynah ؓ once said:

كَانَ العُلَمَاءُ فِيمَا مَضَى يَكْتُبُ بَعْضُهُمْ إِلَى بَعْضٍ بِهَؤُلَاءِ الكَلِمَاتِ: مَنْ أَصْلَحَ سَرِيرَتَهُ، أَصْلَحَ اللهُ عَلَانِيَتَهُ، وَمَنْ أَصْلَحَ مَا بَيْنَهُ وَبَيْنَ اللهِ، أَصْلَحَ اللهُ مَا بَيْنَهُ وَبَيْنَ النَّاسِ، وَمَنْ عَمِلَ لِآخِرَتِهِ، كَفَاهُ اللهُ أَمْرَ دُنْيَاهُ

In the days of old, scholars used to exchange letters, sharing these profound words among themselves: "Whoever rectifies their innermost affairs, Allah will rectify their outward affairs. Whoever rectifies their relationship with Allah, Allah will rectify their relationship with people. And whoever works diligently for their Hereafter, Allah will suffice them in their worldly matters.[142]

---

[141] Al-Bukhārī, *Ṣaḥīḥ al-Bukhārī*.
[142] Ibn Abī al-Dunyā, *Kitāb al-Ikhlāṣ*.

By cultivating a strong bond with Allah ﷻ, you lay a foundation for harmonious interactions with your fellow human beings. Considering this, have you ever paused to contemplate that the bitterness and discord in your relationship with your spouse could be a mere reflection of the bitterness that characterises your relationship with Allah ﷻ? This profound attitude was the lens through which our predecessors viewed their disputes with others and the adversities they encountered in every facet of life. They realised that a strain in one's relationship with Allah ﷻ will cast a shadow on one's relationship with people.

Al-Ḥasan al-Baṣrī, a renowned scholar of the heart, once humbly acknowledged:

وَاللهِ إِنِّي لَأَعْلَمُ ذَنْبِي فِي خُلُقِ زَوْجَتِي وَفِي خُلُقِ دَابَّتِي

By Allah, I truly recognise my own transgression when I witness a change in the behaviour of my spouse and even in the disposition of my riding animal.

Ibn Sīrīn said:

إِنِّي لَأَعْرِفُ الذَّنْبَ الَّذِي حُمِّلَ عَلَيَّ بِهِ الدَّيْنُ. مَا هُوَ؟ قُلْتُ لِرَجُلٍ مِنْ أَرْبَعِينَ سَنَةٍ: يَا مُفْلِس!

I know of the act that plunged me into debt. It was my mockery of an individual four decades ago, as I said to him, "You're penniless."

Commenting on this, Abū Sulaymān al-Darānī said:

قَلَّتْ ذُنُوبُهُمْ فَعَرَفُوا مِنْ أَيْنَ يُؤْتَوْنَ، وَكَثُرَتْ ذُنُوبِي وَذُنُوبُكَ فَلَيْسَ نَدْرِي مِنْ أَيْنَ نُؤْتَى

The scarcity of their sins allowed them to pinpoint the origin of their pain. In contrast, our sins are so many, leaving us oblivious to the source of our anguish.

This awareness and self-reflection came because they truly recognised that *"whatever calamity befalls you then it is because of what your hands have earned"*[143] and were aware that for "whoever fears Allah (or 'has taqwā of Allah') – He will make his matters easy for him."

Ultimately, we are all still human. We will make mistakes from time to time; we all have shortcomings, weaknesses and desires that call us. Does that mean that the happiness of a newly formed couple will be snatched away each and every time they fall prey to a sinful impulse? No, happiness can still exist, albeit with one crucial condition.

Allah ﷻ said:

وَأَنِ اسْتَغْفِرُوا رَبَّكُمْ ثُمَّ تُوبُوا إِلَيْهِ يُمَتِّعْكُمْ مَتَاعًا حَسَنًا إِلَىٰ أَجَلٍ مُسَمًّى

Seek forgiveness from your Lord and repent to Him, and He will give you a good and true enjoyment for a specified term.[144]

The condition for contentment is therefore tawbah – turning back to Allah ﷻ in sincere penitence.

In the midst of occasional conflicts within their household, the exceptional couple approaches the situation with unparalleled introspection. Rather than resorting to blame or pointing fingers, they embark on a shared quest to uncover the root cause of their discord. They earnestly examine themselves, questioning their own flaws, character deficiencies, and any sinful or harmful behaviours that may have contributed to the strain on their marital bond. The husband may sit with himself and reflect, thinking or saying "Yes, this week, I have fallen short in this aspect. I did this…I did that." The wife in such

[143] *Al-Shūrā*, 42:30.
[144] *Hūd*, 11:3.

a relationship does the exact same, and they then both find themselves saying, "O Allah ﷻ, pardon me and pardon us." In response to their genuine repentance, Allah's Mercy descends upon them, effortlessly dissolving the tension and negativity that had clouded their relationship.

One brother recounted a rift with his spouse that caused him to abruptly depart from his home, and seek peace within the sanctuary of the mosque. Yet upon arrival, an unfamiliar restlessness hindered his composure. Despite fervently reciting the verses of the Qur'an and immersing himself in the remembrance of Allah ﷻ, an unseen force impelled him to return to his abode. Yielding to this urge, he retraced his steps, only to be welcomed by his wife, adorned with a gentle smile. "You have returned," she exclaimed with certitude. He replied in affirmation, acknowledging her conviction. She then revealed, "I knew that you would come back, because in your absence, I diligently sought forgiveness through istighfār."

Putting this principle into practice

When it comes to marriages, family life, or any other meaningful relationship you have with others, whenever a rift occurs, you might want to consider your relationship with Allah ﷻ first. It may be the case that you need to strengthen your resolve against sins, as they have consequences that run deep. Oftentimes, the solution might not be visiting a counsellor to resolve marital problems or a strained relationship at the first hurdle. Instead, it could simply be a case of genuinely repenting to Allah ﷻ, mending your ways, and realigning yourself with the framework Allah has blessed us with.

This of course is no magical recipe, for sometimes there are an array of factors that are involved. You, however, are only responsible for what you can do, and repentance and reformation is an open door that benefits everyone.

Unaccounted sins will catch up with you sooner or later. It is a debt that must be paid. Rather than simply demanding a change, invite the change you want to see in your spouse by rectifying yourself first.

CHAPTER FOURTEEN

On disciplining emotions

وَلْكَـٰظِمِينَ لْغَيْظَ

And those who control their anger.[145]

This is part of a verse that describes the people of taqwā in which Allah ﷻ says:

وَسَارِعُوٓا إِلَىٰ مَغْفِرَةٍ مِّن رَّبِّكُمْ وَجَنَّةٍ عَرْضُهَا
لسَّمَـٰوَٰتُ وَلْأَرْضُ أُعِدَّتْ لِلْمُتَّقِينَ

And hasten towards forgiveness from your Lord and a Paradise as vast as the Heavens and the Earth, prepared for those mindful of Allah.

لَّذِينَ يُنفِقُونَ فِى لسَّرَّآءِ وَلضَّرَّآءِ وَلْكَـٰظِمِينَ لْغَيْظَ
وَلْعَافِينَ عَنِ لنَّاسِ وَللَّهُ يُحِبُّ لْمُحْسِنِينَ

They are those who donate in prosperity and adversity, and those who control their anger, and pardon others. And Allah loves the good-doers.[146]

---

[145] *Āl ʿImrān*, 3:134.
[146] *Āl ʿImrān*, 3:134.

Anger and its consequences can be a truly terminal disease for marital contentment. A variety of studies from different marriage researchers unanimously found that the major predictor of divorce was not disappointment over finances, lack of sexual attraction or love, but the way couples handle their disagreements and anger.

When dealing with community issues at grassroots level, we struggle to count the number of men who find themselves in a bind because of yet another divorce that had been issued out of anger. Filled with regret after they have sobered up, they plead for an arbitrator to get involved: does the divorce count, was the anger strong enough that it invalidated the pronouncement of divorce? Does this outburst of anger mean that the man cannot take his wife back as his spouse again? Suffice to say, anger has extremely grave consequences.

Similarly, we have witnessed a huge number of wives who have landed themselves and their families in deplorable situations because her anger pushed her to make a few phone calls that she fast comes to regret, as acting in anger meant that certain government agencies are now inextricably involved in her marital problems. This is something that now she cannot easily undo, as the damage is done.

In relation to anger, there are a couple of things we must bear in mind:

Caveat 1: Anger (not rage, or tantrums) is a normal human emotion that can be healthy when channelled productively. Experiencing anger is a way our bodies signal something is wrong and that we need to "adjust fire". Anger is the tip of action, and people should rightly feel angry when threatened, wronged, persecuted or when witnessing injustice. When we feel angry watching a vulnerable person being abused or people's rights being taken away from them, anger spurs us into action to overcome a threat or right a wrong. Many matters would not get done if it was not for anger, and the unjust would run around with impunity. If properly managed within the right context, anger can be an indispensable, valued ally.

Caveat 2: The Prophet ﷺ got angry. He said:

إِنَّمَا أَنَا بَشَرٌ أَغْضَبُ كَمَا يَغْضَبُ الْبَشَرُ

I am a human being, I get angry like all humans do.[147]

ʿĀ'ishah ﷺ described the physical impact anger had on the Messenger of Allah ﷺ:

بَيْنَهُمَا عِرْقٌ يَدُرُّهُ الغَضَبُ لَا يُرَى ذَلِكَ العِرْقُ إِلَّا أَنْ يدُرُّهُ الغَضَبُ

Between his eyebrows was a vein, its pulsating presence fuelled by anger and only ever appearing when he was angered.[148]

The anger of the Prophet ﷺ was unique in that it only emerged when the boundaries of Allah's rights were transgressed, rather than for personal reasons. Numerous instances illustrate his displays of anger, even towards those closest to him. One such display of anger was directed towards Usāmah ﷺ after he attempted to intercede on behalf of a Makhzūmī woman who had committed theft in order to spare her from punishment. Another example reveals his anger directed at ʿAlī ﷺ, upon witnessing him adorned in a silk garment – a violation of the Shariah, as men are forbidden from wearing silk. Additionally, his frustration was evident when Muʿādh ﷺ prolonged the prayer, causing undue hardship for his people. These instances and others exemplify how the Prophet's anger was never self-centred, but rather stemmed from his unwavering devotion to preserving Allah's rights.

---

[147] Ibn Ḥanbal, *Musnad Aḥmad.*

[148] Al-Bayhaqī, *Al-Sunan al-Kubrā li al-Bayhaqī.*

Secondly, as someone in control of himself, his anger worked for him, never against him. It never led him to act recklessly or engage in destructive behaviour, such as throwing or breaking things, or resorting to profanity. Such impulsive and uncontrolled reactions were conspicuously absent from his exemplary character.

Managing anger

Learning to manage anger is one of the most important life skills we can gift ourselves. We can divide this into three levels:

I. To work towards anger minimisation

The essence of ḥilm (clemency or forbearance) is about not becoming easily triggered by other people's behaviour or stressful situations. People who have this characteristic exude an outer calm that reflects their inner state – their nervous system is not easily riled up as they are internally grounded and enjoy a sense of perpetual serenity. These are the people whose internal constancy stays strong, and they are not moved by the petty, trivial or mundane annoyances of life.

On one occasion the Messenger of Allah ﷺ was with one of his wives when another one of his wives sent him a plate of food. The wife with whom he was with intentionally struck the plate in jealousy, causing it to fall and break. The Prophet ﷺ calmly gathered the broken pieces of the plate and began collecting the food, saying, "Your mother was jealous, your mother was jealous"[149] – as if to say do not think bad of her, for jealousy is a natural tendency that affects us all. Furthermore, she is not just anyone, but your own mother, deserving of respect and compassion.

[149] Al-Bukhārī, *Ṣaḥīḥ al-Bukhārī*.

According to another narration in the collection of al-Tirmidhī ﷬, the Prophet ﷺ said, "Food with food and a dish with a dish."[150]

What is most remarkable are the words of ʿĀ'ishah ﷞ commenting on the demeanour of the Prophet ﷺ during this incident, as she said:

فَمَا رَأَيْتُ ذَلِكَ فِي وَجْهِ رَسُولِ اللهِ صَلَّى اللهُ عَلَيْهِ وَسَلَّمَ

I did not see any anger in the face of the Prophet ﷺ.

The benefit of such people also spreads wide, as they are able to pull people *into* their calm, instead of allowing people to pull *them* into their storm. Undoubtedly, the initial phase of anger minimisation is a journey that demands time and is marked by inevitable missteps and imperfections. Therefore, in instances where one falters or falls short, it is crucial to remember and embrace the second stage of conquering anger.

II. Train yourself to keep reactions at bay when triggered

This is the understanding of the Hadith that advises us to "not become angry".[151] The scholar and Hadith commentator al-Khaṭṭābī ﷬ understood this Hadith to mean:

لَا تَقبَلْ مَا يَأْمُرُكَ بِهِ الغَضَبُ وَيَحْمِلُكَ عَلَيْهِ مِنَ الأَقْوَالِ وَالأَفْعَالِ

Do not carry out the dictates of anger that are usually expressed via speech and actions.

Managing reactions effectively can be accomplished through the following approaches:

[150] Al-Tirmidhī, *Jāmiʿ al-Tirmidhī*.
[151] Al-Bukhārī, *Ṣaḥīḥ al-Bukhārī*.

1. Seeking refuge in Allah ﷻ from Shayṭān

As parents, we bear the responsibility of safeguarding our homes – not only from physical threats, but also from the spiritual enemy of Allah ﷻ and humanity, Iblīs (the Devil). This sacred trust places a significant burden on our shoulders, and we must be cautious not to betray this responsibility.

Allah ﷻ instructs us:

وَإِمَّا يَنزَغَنَّكَ مِنَ الشَّيْطَانِ نَزْغٌ فَاسْتَعِذْ بِاللَّهِ

And if an evil suggestion comes to you from Shayṭān, then seek refuge in Allah.[152]

The great exegete al-Ṭabarī said, "'If an evil suggestion comes to you from Shayṭān…' means 'if Shayṭān angers you…'"[153]

The Companion Sulaymān ibn Ṣurad h said, "Two men argued in the presence of the Prophet ﷺ while we were sitting with him. One of them was insulting the other, his face turning red with anger. The Prophet ﷺ said, 'I know a word that, if he were to say it, the anger would leave him. If he said, "Aʿūdhu bi Allåh min al-Shayṭān al-Rajīm" (I seek refuge with Allah from Shayṭān, the accursed) his anger would dissipate.'"[154]

While this method of seeking refuge in Allah ﷻ during moments of anger may seem simple, it is important to acknowledge that not everyone may find it easy to utter this phrase in the heat of the moment. This ability is intricately connected to the principle preceding it, which is taqwā, or God-consciousness. Only those who possess taqwā, who are deeply aware of their relationship with Allah ﷻ and who constantly strive to please Him will find themselves inspired by Him to utter this statement.

---

[152] *Al-Aʿrāf*, 7:200.

[153] Al-Ṭabarī, *Tafsīr al-Ṭabarī*.

[154] Al-Bukhārī, *Ṣaḥīḥ al-Bukhārī;* Muslim, *Ṣaḥīḥ Muslim*.

Allah ﷻ, in His infinite wisdom, states in the Qur'an:

إِنَّ الَّذِينَ اتَّقَوْا إِذَا مَسَّهُمْ طَائِفٌ مِنَ الشَّيْطَانِ
تَذَكَّرُوا فَإِذَا هُمْ مُبْصِرُونَ

Indeed, those who fear Allah – when an impulse touches them from Shayṭān, they remember [Him] and at once they have insight.[155]

2. Perform wuḍū'

Once, while Muʿāwiyah ؓ was delivering a sermon, a man stood up and said to him, "You are lying." Muʿāwiyah ؓ, feeling angry, descended from the pulpit and went into his house. Shortly after, he emerged with drops of water dripping from his beard. He ascended the pulpit once again and addressed the people, saying, "O people, indeed, anger is from Shayṭān, and Shayṭān is from the Fire. So, when any one of you becomes angry, let him extinguish it with water." He then resumed his sermon from where he had left off.[156]

3. Change your posture

If you are in the throes of an angry outburst, try to change your physical position, as the Prophet ﷺ said:

إِذَا غَضِبَ أَحَدُكُمْ وَهوَ قَائِمٌ فَلْيَجْلِسْ فَإِنْ ذَهَبَ عنْهُ الغَضَبُ وَإِلَّا
فَلْيَضْطَجِعْ

When one of you becomes angry while standing, he should sit down. If the anger leaves him, well and good; otherwise, he should lie down.[157]

---

[155] *Al-Aʿrāf*, 7:201.

[156] Ibn Qutaybah, *ʿUyūn al-Akhbār*.

[157] Ibn Ḥanbal, *Musnad Aḥmad*.

4. Be aware of the harms of unmanaged anger

The short and long-term health problems that have been linked to unmanaged anger include migraines, insomnia, anxiety, depression, and high blood pressure, in addition to the spiritual misery it causes. The true face of anger can be very uncomfortable to look at. Should you see your reflection in a mirror during your moment of rage, you would hate what you see – a clenched jaw, intense eye contact, pupils dilated, furrowed brows, teeth grinding, nostrils flared, lips that have thinned, and a fiery, red face. Shayṭān could not be happier when you are in this state, as at that second, you are his helpless puppet.

5. Frequently refresh your knowledge on the virtues of anger management

It is crucial to recognise that anger management is not just a personal endeavour, but an act of worship that holds immense rewards. Interestingly, the greater the intensity of anger, the more significant the position attained by those who master its restraint.

The Prophet ﷺ said:

الصُّرَعةُ كُلُّ الصُّرَعةِ: الرَّجُلُ يَغضَبُ فيَشتَدُّ غَضَبُه،
وَيَحمَرُّ وَجْهُه، وَيَقشَعِرُّ شَعَرُه، فيَصْرَعُ غَضَبَه

The truly strong individuals are those who, even in the face of intense anger that causes their face to redden and their hair to stand on end, possess the ability to conquer and subdue their rage.[158]

He ﷺ also said:

ومَنْ كَظَم غيْظَهُ وَلَوْ شَاءَ أَنْ يُمْضِيَهُ أَمْضاهُ مَلأَ اللهُ قلْبَهُ يَوْمَ القِيامَةِ رِضًا

And whoever suppresses anger, even though they have the ability

[158] Ibn Ḥanbal, *Musnad Aḥmad.*

> to unleash it, Allah will fill their heart with satisfaction on the Day of Resurrection.[159]

A great reward has also been promised for those who do so, as the following Hadith informs us:

مَنْ كَظَمَ غَيْظًا وَهُوَ قَادِرٌ عَلَى أَنْ يُنْفِذَهُ دَعَاهُ اللهُ عَزَّ وَجَلَّ عَلَى رُؤُوسِ الخَلَائِقِ يَوْمَ القِيَامَةِ حَتَّى يُخَيِّرَهُ اللهُ مِنَ الحُورِ مَا شَاءَ

> Whoever suppresses their anger, even though they have the ability to act upon it, Allah ﷻ will call them on the Day of Judgment in the presence of all creation and grant them the choice of any of the wide-eyed maidens of Paradise they desire.[160]

6. Du'ā'

The impact of *du'ā'* as a transformative tool allows individuals to transcend their primal instincts and overcome the turbulent waves of anger cannot be emphasised enough. The Prophet Muhammad ﷺ exemplified this by consistently supplicating to Allah ﷻ, seeking His guidance and assistance in attaining the noblest conduct, including the mastery of anger appropriation and management. He would raise his hands to the sky, earnestly invoking Allah ﷻ:

اللَّهُمَّ بِعِلْمِكَ الْغَيْبَ وَقُدْرَتِكَ عَلَى الْخَلْقِ أَحْيِنِي مَا عَلِمْتَ الْحَيَاةَ خَيْرًا لِي وَتَوَفَّنِي إِذَا عَلِمْتَ الْوَفَاةَ خَيْرًا لِي اللَّهُمَّ وَأَسْأَلُكَ خَشْيَتَكَ فِي الْغَيْبِ وَالشَّهَادَةِ وَأَسْأَلُكَ كَلِمَةَ الْحَقِّ فِي الرِّضَا وَالْغَضَبِ وَأَسْأَلُكَ الْقَصْدَ فِي الْفَقْرِ وَالْغِنَى وَأَسْأَلُكَ نَعِيمًا لاَ يَنْفَدُ وَأَسْأَلُكَ قُرَّةَ عَيْنٍ لاَ تَنْقَطِعُ وَأَسْأَلُكَ الرِّضَاءَ بَعْدَ الْقَضَاءِ وَأَسْأَلُكَ بَرْدَ الْعَيْشِ بَعْدَ الْمَوْتِ وَأَسْأَلُكَ لَذَّةَ النَّظَرِ إِلَى وَجْهِكَ وَالشَّوْقَ إِلَى لِقَائِكَ فِي غَيْرِ ضَرَّاءَ مُضِرَّةٍ وَلاَ فِتْنَةٍ مُضِلَّةٍ اللَّهُمَّ زَيِّنَّا بِزِينَةِ الإِيمَانِ وَاجْعَلْنَا هُدَاةً مُهْتَدِينَ

---

159 Al-Ṭabarānī, *Mu'jam al-Kabīr li al-Ṭabarānī.*

160 Abū Dāwūd, *Sunan Abū Dāwūd.*

> O Allah, by Your knowledge of the unseen and Your power over creation, keep me alive so long as You know that living is good for me and cause me to die when You know that death is better for me. O Allah, cause me to fear You in secret and in public. I ask You to make me true in speech in times of pleasure and of anger. I ask You to grant me moderation in times of wealth and poverty.

And I ask You for everlasting delight and joy that will never cease. I ask You to make me pleased with that which You have decreed and for an easy life after death. I ask You for the sweetness of looking upon Your face and a longing to meet You in a manner that is not due to a harmful calamity or a deviating trial. O Allah, beautify us with the adornment of faith and make us among those who guide and are rightly guided.[161]

Thus far, we have explored two aspects of anger management: the first being the minimisation of anger, and the second emphasising the importance of maintaining control over our reactions when provoked. However, it is crucial to address a third level of anger management, which arises when our reactions overflow, resulting in harm to others.

III. Make amends if you fail to control your anger

After experiencing a bout of anger and regaining composure, it is essential to embark on the journey of rectification. This entails taking responsibility for the harm caused and seeking reconciliation with those affected by your anger. It begins with sincerely apologising to those who have suffered the consequences of your anger and earnestly seeking their forgiveness. Simultaneously, introspection is imperative in making amends, as you must reflect upon the triggers that led to that moment of anger. By carefully examining these triggers, you can gain

[161] Al-Nasā'ī, *As-Sunan al-Ṣughrā li al-Nasā'ī*.

valuable insight into your own vulnerabilities and establish safeguards to prevent the repetition of negative behaviour patterns in the future.

Putting this principle into practice

Do not make decisions when you are angry

Decisions made in times of anger will be highly influenced by your fleeting emotions at that passing time. We often hear the phrases "blinded by love", "paralysed by fear", or "ill with stress". Do not make promises when you are happy, and do not make decisions when you are angry. The best way to react when you are angry is to not react at all. What might appear rational in that heated moment will likely seem to be pure insanity after just a few hours have passed, prompting you to question, "Why on earth did I think in such a way?" or "Why on earth did I do that?"

Diffuse the anger before it escalates

We all understand that prevention is better than cure, and defusing a situation in its early stages is better than trying to recover from its full consequences. Be sensitive by reading your spouse and their emotional cues. When you can sense that a situation is escalating into an unproductive and emotionally charged territory, attempt to step away from the situation and allow yourselves to both calm down separately before you come together to discuss the situation in an effective way. Sometimes the situation will not have a neat resolution, but the least that can be done is to handle discussions around it with sensitivity and care.

CHAPTER FIFTEEN

On exercising forgiveness

وَلْعَافِينَ عَنِ لنَّاسِ

And those who pardon others.[162]

The topic of forgiveness is closely intertwined with our previous discussions on reconciliation. Although there can be forgiveness without reconciliation, there cannot be true reconciliation without forgiveness. In the context of marriage, the inability to genuinely forgive one another can lead to a destructive cycle of retaliation and a constant desire to "even the score" with your spouse.We are all imperfect beings who are prone to making mistakes that can hurt or disappoint our loved ones. Forgiveness serves as a crucial mechanism for repairing relationships, enabling them to emerge stronger than before. However, for forgiveness to have a transformative impact, it requires the forgiving party to genuinely let go of resentment and the guilty party to make sincere efforts to avoid repeating their hurtful behaviour.

[162] *Āl ʿImrān*, 3:134.

But why pardon?

Many find themselves ensnared in the grips of anger, resentment, and bitterness towards those who have inflicted pain upon them. In truth, each one of us feels hurt by someone and yearns for a resolution to that hurt. Yet, the act of forgiving and mending wounds demands patience, as the magnitude of the hurt endured corresponds to the time required for the balm of forgiveness to take effect. However, as your comprehension of the rewards involved deepens, your willingness to grant pardon will expand to become vastly more attainable, even in the face of grievous transgressions. On that note, allow me to present a glimpse of what awaits those who consciously choose to extend clemency to others.

Allah ﷻ declares:

وَمَا عِنْدَ اللَّهِ خَيْرٌ وَأَبْقَى لِلَّذِينَ آمَنُوا وَعَلَى رَبِّهِمْ يَتَوَكَّلُونَ. وَالَّذِينَ يَجْتَنِبُونَ
كَبَائِرَ الْإِثْمِ وَالْفَوَاحِشَ وَإِذَا مَا غَضِبُوا هُمْ يَغْفِرُونَ

But what is with Allah is better and more lasting for those who have believed and upon their Lord rely. And those who avoid the major sins and immoralities, and when they are angry, they forgive.[163] *Allah ﷻ also said:*

وَلَمَنْ صَبَرَ وَغَفَرَ إِنَّ ذَلِكَ لَمِنْ عَزْمِ الْأُمُورِ

And whoever endures patiently and forgives – s urely this is a resolve to aspire to.[164]

The Qur'an also informs us that:

وَأَنْ تَعْفُوا أَقْرَبُ لِلتَّقْوَى

And to forego is nearer to righteousness.[165]

---

[163] *Āl 'Imrān*, 3:134.
[164] *Al-Shūrā*, 42:43.
[165] *Al-Baqarah* 2:237.

Furthermore, is it not the case that we fervently hope that our own repentance is accepted, and that our countless wrongdoings are wiped away by Allah's pardon? If this is the case, then how can we expect from Allah ﷻ what we are unwilling to extend to others? In fact, if we self reflect, people's imperfections and shortcomings towards us, however regrettable, pale in comparison to our own deficiencies towards Allah ﷻ. After all, their errors are directed at mere humans and fallible mortals, while our transgressions are directed at the Immortal and Everlasting. Yet, despite this stark reality, Allah ﷻ, in His divine benevolence, still pardons and forgives. So who are we, mere mortals, to stubbornly insist otherwise? This was the realisation that swiftly dawned upon Abū Bakr رضي الله عنه when he was wronged.

When our mother ʿĀ'ishah رضي الله عنها was maligned by the hypocrites in what would be later known as the event of ʿĀ'ishah رضي الله عنها, a relative of Abū Bakr رضي الله عنه – Misṭaḥ ibn Uthāthah رضي الله عنه – did not play the ideal role in defending ʿĀ'ishah رضي الله عنها. Misṭaḥ رضي الله عنه was poor and was living off the generosity of Abū Bakr رضي الله عنه, but after seeing how Misṭaḥ رضي الله عنه had spoken about his daughter, Abū Bakr رضي الله عنه said, "By Allah, never again will I spend on Misṭaḥ!"

After ʿĀ'ishah رضي الله عنها was exonerated by Allah in the Qur'an, verses were revealed commenting on Abū Bakr's oath to no longer spend on his relative, reading:

وَلَا يَأْتَلِ أُولُو الْفَضْلِ مِنكُمْ وَالسَّعَةِ أَنْ يُؤْتُوا أُولِي الْقُرْبَىٰ وَالْمَسَاكِينَ
وَالْمُهَاجِرِينَ فِي سَبِيلِ اللَّهِ وَلْيَعْفُوا وَلْيَصْفَحُوا أَلَا تُحِبُّونَ أَنْ يَغْفِرَ اللَّهُ
لَكُمْ وَاللَّهُ غَفُورٌ رَحِيمٌ

And let not those of virtue among you and wealth swear not to give [aid] to their relatives and the needy and the emigrants for the cause of Allah and let them pardon and overlook. Would you not like that Allah should forgive you? And Allah is Forgiving and Merciful.[166]

[166] *Al-Nūr*, 24:22.

Without a backward glance or the faintest hint of hesitation, Abū Bakr ☙ exclaimed:

$$\text{بَلَى وَاللَّهِ إِنِّي أُحِبُّ أَنْ يَغْفِرَ اللَّهُ لِي وَاللَّهِ لاَ أَنْزِعُهَا مِنْهُ أَبَدًا}$$

Yes, by Allah! I love that Allah forgives me. By Allah, I will never stop spending on him ever again.[167]

Those most deserving of our forgiveness are our parents, spouse, children, siblings, relatives, and fellow Muslims with whom we share the unbreakable bond of *īmān*. It is essential to embrace their apologies, grant them our pardon, and release any lingering resentment. Reflection over the verse above should enable you to forgive all those who wrong you as you seek to gain the blessings of the verse that 'Abdullāh ibn al-Mubārak ☙ aptly described by saying:

$$\text{هَذِهِ أَرْجَى آيَةٍ فِي كِتَابِ اللهِ}$$

It is the most hopeful verse in the entire Qur'an.[168]

Regardless of your virtue to others, Allah ☙ can never be surpassed; no matter what goodness you confer upon people, Allah's bounty will always outshine and overwhelm. To demonstrate this, the Prophet ☙ informed us of a merchant who used to offer loans to people. Whenever he saw the distress of a debtor who was facing financial difficulty, he would say to his assistant:

$$\text{تَجَاوَزْ لَعَلَّ اللهُ يَتَجَاوَزُ عَنَّا}$$

Waive the debt so that perhaps Allah will waive our sins.

The Messenger of Allah ☙ informed us that:

---

[167] Al-Bukhārī, *Saḥīḥ al-Bukhārī*.
[168] Muslim, *Ṣaḥīḥ Muslim*.

فَلَقِيَ اللَّهَ فَتَجَاوَزَ عَنْهُ

He met Allah, and Allah pardoned him.[169]

Why ask for pardon?

With the above under consideration, it is essential to recognise that virtue extends beyond merely bestowing forgiveness upon those who have caused you harm. Equally virtuous is the act of seeking pardon from those whom you have caused pain, acknowledging your faults with humility, and earnestly striving for reconciliation. This is particularly true in the realm of marriage, as your spouse stands amongst the closest and most cherished individuals in your life. The Prophet ﷺ said:

أَلَا أُخبِرُكُم بِنِسَائِكُم فِي الجَنَّةِ؟ كُلُّ وَدُودٍ وَلُودٍ إِذَا غَضِبَت أَو أُسِيءَ إِلَيهَا أَو غَضِبَ زَوجُهَا قَالَت: هَذِه يَدِي فِي يَدِكَ لَا أَكْتَحِلُ بِغُمضٍ حتَّى تَرضَى

> Shall I not inform you about your women in Paradise? They are affectionate and fertile, whom, if they become angry, or are wronged, or if their husbands become angry, they say, "This is my hand in your hand. I will not sleep until you are pleased."[170]

Levels of forgiveness

In the realm of forgiveness, there are three distinct levels that manifest varying degrees of virtue and magnanimity. These levels can be seen as progressive stages, each encompassing a higher degree of virtuous behaviour towards the wrongdoer:

[169] Al-Bukhārī, *Ṣaḥīḥ al-Bukhārī;* Muslim, *Ṣaḥīḥ Muslim.*
[170] Al-Nasā'ī, *As-Sunan al-Ṣughrā li al-Nasā'ī.*

1. Withholding retaliation

The initial level of forgiveness is that of refraining from seeking retribution or inflicting harm upon the one who has wronged you. It involves letting go of the desire for revenge and choosing not to retaliate. This act of restraint demonstrates a commendable strength of character, as it requires one to deliberately reject the urge to respond in accordance with the human desire for tit-for-tat retaliation.

2. Pardoning

Moving beyond merely abstaining from punishment, the next level involves a conscious decision to avoid bringing up the wrongdoing or reminding the wrongdoer of their offence. Through doing so, your grip on the past is relinquished, freeing you from the heavy chains of resentment.

3. To do good to the wrongdoer

The highest level of forgiveness entails actively treating the wrongdoer with kindness and goodwill. This level of forgiveness transcends the mere absence of punishment or pardoning and actively seeks to repair and restore the relationship with proactive acts of kindness.

Interestingly, all three of these levels are captured in a single Qur'anic verse, where, after promising the people of piety Paradise, Allah ﷻ describes several of their traits, including:

الَّذِينَ يُنفِقُونَ فِى السَّرَّآءِ وَالضَّرَّآءِ وَالْكَـٰظِمِينَ الْغَيْظَ وَالْعَافِينَ عَنِ النَّاسِ
وَاللَّهُ يُحِبُّ الْمُحْسِنِينَ

Those who spend [in the cause of Allah] during ease and hardship and who restrain anger (the first level) and who pardon the people (the second level) –

and Allah loves the doers of good (the third level).[171]

The barriers to forgiveness

Shayṭān, being the persistent adversary lurks on every potential path of goodness and virtue, waiting to ambush us and divert us from Allah's Pleasure. Let us delve into the dialogue that typically unfolds between an individual and Shayṭān when they consider accepting an apology and extending forgiveness.

Shayṭān will cunningly suggest, "Suppressing your anger and refraining from retaliation will only breed resentment and cause rancour to ferment within your heart. It is better to unleash your anger and vent to your frustrations in a healthy manner!" How do we respond? Naturally, with the Hadith of the Prophet ﷺ:

مَا تَجَرَّعَ عَبْدٌ مِنْ جَرْعَةٍ أَحَبَّ إِلَى اللهِ مِنْ جَرْعَةِ غَيْظٍ يَكْظِمُهَا عَبْدٌ مَا كَظَمَهَا إِلَّا لِلهِ إِلَّا مَلَأَ جَوْفَهُ إِيمَانًا

There is no swallowing which is more beloved to Allah than the swallowing of anger for the sake of Allah. Whenever one does so, Allah will most certainly fill him with *īmān*.[172]

Notice the difference between Shayṭān's narrative – "suppressing anger will fill you with poison" and the Prophetic path – "suppressing it will fill you with *īmān*."

Should you succeed in suppressing your rage, ensure that you follow this difficult period with a calm and healthy period of introspection thereafter. Shayṭān, relentless as ever, will soon reappear and employ a second tactic, saying, "Look, you have so many other good deeds! You pray at night, read Qur'an, take part in circles of knowledge, so surely Allah will pardon you for this one fallout! What's the urgency to reconcile?"

---

171 *Āl ʿImrān*, 3:134.

172 Ibn Ḥanbal, *Musnad Aḥmad*.

How do we respond to this argument? Again, with the Hadith of the Prophet ﷺ:

تُعْرَضُ الأَعْمَالُ فِي كُلِّ اثْنَيْنِ وَخَمِيسٍ فَيَغْفِرُ اللهُ لِكُلِّ امْرِئٍ لا يُشْرِكُ بِاللهِ شَيْئًا إِلاَّ امْرَءًا كَانَتْ بَيْنَهُ وَبَيْنَ أَخِيهِ شَحْنَاءُ فَيَقُولُ: اتْرُكُوا هذَيْنِ حَتَّى يَصْطَلِحَا

The deeds of people are presented to Allah every Monday and Thursday and Allah forgives the sins of every Muslim who does not associate a partner with Allah, with the exception of two people who have fallen out. It is said, "Do not forgive their sins until they reconcile."[173]

So, despite one's "many good deeds", this "one fall out" may prevent one from having their sins forgiven.

Undeterred, Shayṭān will refuse to relent and continues his insidious persuasion, suggesting, "Alright, do not retaliate and seek reconciliation, but perhaps you can delay it. Give it some time, maybe a year or so."

How do we respond to this? Once more, with the Hadith of the Prophet ﷺ:

مَنْ هَجَرَ أَخَاهُ سَنَةً فَهُوَ كَسَفْكِ دَمِهِ

Whoever boycotts his brother for over a year, then it is as if he has spilt his blood.[174]

Shayṭān, adapting his approach once again, will say, "Very well; not a year, but give it a week or so. Surely you both need to cool down!" How do we respond? As always, with the Hadith of the Prophet ﷺ:

---

[173] Muslim, *Ṣaḥīḥ Muslim*.

[174] Abū Dāwūd, *Sunan Abū Dāwūd*.

لاَ يَحِلُّ لِمُسْلِمٍ أَنْ يَهْجُرَ أَخَاهُ فَوْقَ ثَلاَثٍ، فَمَنْ هَجَرَ فَوْقَ ثَلاَثٍ فَمَاتَ دَخَلَ النَّارَ

It is not permissible for a Muslim to boycott his brother for over three days, and whoever does so and then dies, will enter the Fire.[175]

Shayṭān's faltering voice grows desperate, exclaiming, "Do not retaliate, hold onto resentment, or even allow it to persist for a mere week. But, at the very least, demand that the other person initiates the apology!"

How do we respond to this? The Hadith of the Prophet ﷺ forever repels such demonic whispers:

وخَيْرُهُما الَّذِي يَبْدَأُ بِالسَّلاَمِ

The best of the two who have fallen out is the one who initiates *salām* first.[176]

"Ah! But what if he rejects your apology?", Shayṭān's voice will suggest, attempting to shake your resolve, "Your sincere efforts to reconcile will be in vain!"

Once more, respond with the Hadith of the Prophet ﷺ:

لاَ يَحِلُّ لِمُؤْمِنٍ أَنْ يَهْجُرَ مُؤْمِنًا فَوقَ ثَلاَثٍ فإِنْ مَرَّتْ بِهِ ثَلاَثٌ فَلْيَلْقَهُ فَلْيُسَلِّمْ عَلَيْهِ، فَإِنْ رَدَّ عَلَيْهِ السَّلامَ فَقَدِ اشْتَرَكَا في الأَجْرِ وَإِنْ لَمْ يَرُدَّ عَلَيْهِ فَقَدْ بَاءَ بِالإِثْمِ وَخَرَجَ المُسَلِّمُ مِنَ الهِجْرَةِ

It is not permissible for a believer to boycott his brother for over three days; therefore if three days pass, let him meet him and give him *salām*. If he responds, then they are both rewarded. But if he rejects him, then only he will be sinful whilst the other has freed himself from blame.[177]

[175] Abū Dāwūd, *Sunan Abū Dāwūd*.
[176] Al-Bukhārī, *Ṣaḥīḥ al-Bukhārī*.
[177] Abū Dāwūd, *Sunan Abū Dāwūd*.

In a final desperate plea, Shayṭān will go to great lengths to prevent us from taking the path to Paradise, begging us to reconsider, whispering, "You will lose all your self-respect if he rejects your apology! Do not humiliate yourself like that!"

Respond, yet again, with the emphatic promise of the Prophet ﷺ who said:

ثَلَاثٌ أُقْسِمُ عَلَيْهِنَّ: مَا نَقَصَ مَالٌ مِنْ صَدَقَةٍ وَمَا زَادَ اللَّهُ عَبْدًا بِعَفْوٍ إِلَّا عِزا وَمَنْ تَوَاضَعَ لِلَّهِ رَفَعَهُ اللَّهُ

There are three things that I swear by: 1 – When one gives wealth in charity, your wealth has not decreased. 2 – When one pardons, Allah will increase you in dignity. 3 – Whoever humbles himself for the sake of Allah, Allah will raise him.[178]

After hearing about this, one who insists on continuing to shun his fellow Muslim and is unwilling to pick up the phone and extend an apology may be displaying traits of arrogance or a hardened heart. Tragically, the allure of Paradise or the fear of Hellfire might not be potent enough to spur them into taking prompt action to reconcile. It may also be that the emotional wounds run deep, which hinders their ability to rationally process the advice and act upon it swiftly. Regardless of the reason, rise above these hurdles, humiliate Shayṭān, and liberate your aching soul! Take charge of your actions and do not let resentment or stubbornness be your guide. Instead, pick up the phone, extend a heartfelt apology, and eliminate every obstacle in your way before you are brought to stand in the court of Allah ﷻ. We all carry burdens that we will be held accountable for, so do not add to this burden by being someone who is "difficult to repair".

Al-Shaʿbī ﵀ beautifully contrasted the difference between forgiving, noble souls and their stubborn, debased counterparts, saying:

[178] Muslim, *Ṣaḥīḥ Muslim*.

إِنَّ كِرَامَ النَّاسِ أَسْرَعُهُمْ مَوَدَّةً وَأَبْطَؤُهُمْ عَدَاوَةً مِثْلَ الكُوبِ مِنَ الفِضَّةِ
يُبْطِئُ الِانْكِسَارَ وَيُسْرِعُ الِانْجِبَارَ، وَإِنَّ لِئَامَ النَّاسِ أَبْطَؤُهُمْ مَوَدَّةً وَأَسْرَعُهُمْ
عَدَاوَةً مِثْلَ الكُوبِ مِنَ الفَخَّارِ يُسْرِعُ الِانْكِسَارَ وَيُبْطِئُ الِانْجِبَارَ

> The honourable are the quickest to reconcile and the slowest to
> fall out. They are like silver vessels – hard to break and easy to
> repair. As for the ill-mannered, they are the slowest of all people
> to make up and the quickest to make enemies. They are like glass
> vessels – easy to break and hard to repair.[179]

Putting this principle into practice

Realign your attitude towards forgiveness in marriage

The difference between the presence of forgiveness and its
absence in a marriage can be likened to the difference between
adhering to the letter or the spirit of a law. In a healthy marriage,
the essence of happiness lies in acknowledging and accepting
each other's imperfections, which paves the way for forgiveness.
Contrastingly, approaching a marriage solely through thinking
about one's rights and obligations without room for mistakes or
forgiveness creates a rigid environment that hampers growth
and genuine connection.

Imagine a couple who have meticulously outlined their individual rights and obligations, etching them onto a metaphorical
wall, dutifully reciting and enforcing these rules every day. This
approach is far removed from the essence of marriage and the
reality of human relationships. When the understanding of
marriage is reduced to a legalistic framework focused solely on
rights and responsibilities, the partnership begins to falter.

The ability to forgive and seek forgiveness is generally considered to be one of the most important factors that affect

---

[179] Ibn Ḥibbān, *Rawḍah al-ʿUqalāʾ*.

relationship longevity and contentment. To forgive is to set a prisoner free and discover that the prisoner was you.

Slow down and process words before reacting

At the heart of many bitter arguments between couples is the tendency to jump to – and subsequently act upon – conclusions, many of which can be very inaccurate. You will never regret the time you take to actively slow down and think through how you should respond to conflict. Press the pause button on the many hurtful things you would like to say and the accusations you wish to make. Anger not only dismantles the goodwill of a couple, but oftentimes causes a communication breakdown in real time, thereby preventing reconciliation. Words spoken in this time can never be retracted, even if you apologise afterwards.

In these moments, disengage from the situation if you need to. And if you can stay, then listen with the intention to truly understand, not merely to prepare your counter-argument. There is always something else lingering underneath anger – and this is oftentimes the unmet needs of your spouse.

You may find indications that your spouse is feeling neglected and unloved. The anger might be masking deep-seated pain or frustration that is being inappropriately expressed through vitriol. Take time and space to calm down and think things through if you need to, and never allow anger to hijack the entire conversation. Slow down and process everything that is being expressed so this unpleasant encounter can be a catalyst for increased understanding, communication and – in shā' Allāh – love between you both.

CHAPTER SIXTEEN

On returning to Divine solutions

فَرُدُّوهُ إِلَى اللَّهِ وَالرَّسُولِ إِنْ كُنْتُمْ تُؤْمِنُونَ بِاللَّهِ وَالْيَوْمِ الْآخِرِ

Then return it back to Allah & His Messenger if you believe in Allah and the Last Day.[180]

It is essential to recognise that no opinion, regardless of its source, can be considered infallible except for that which has been revealed by Allah ﷻ and conveyed by His Messenger ﷺ. This principle applies irrespective of whether an opinion is given by a scholar, a political authority, a respected community member, or any other individual or body.

Asserting that a particular person's statement settles a matter beyond debate and renders all other opinions incorrect implies that said person shares an equal platform with the Prophet Muhammad ﷺ – a Prophet who received divine revelation from Allah ﷻ – and essentially contradicts the fundamentals of Islam.

Allah ﷻ declares:

[180] *Al-Nisā'*, 4:59.

وَمَا اخْتَلَفْتُمْ فِيهِ مِنْ شَيْءٍ فَحُكْمُهُ إِلَى اللَّهِ

And in anything over which you disagree – its ruling is [to be referred] to Allah.[181]

Allah ﷻ also states:

فَلَا وَرَبِّكَ لَا يُؤْمِنُونَ حَتَّى يُحَكِّمُوكَ فِيمَا شَجَرَ بَيْنَهُمْ ثُمَّ لَا يَجِدُوا فِي
أَنْفُسِهِمْ حَرَجًا مِمَّا قَضَيْتَ وَيُسَلِّمُوا تَسْلِيمًا

But no, by your Lord, they will not believe until they make you, [O Muhammad], judge concerning their disputes, and then find within themselves no discomfort from what you have judged and submit in [full, willing] submission.[182]

Allah ﷻ cautions us that:

وَمَا كَانَ لِمُؤْمِنٍ وَلَا مُؤْمِنَةٍ إِذَا قَضَى اللَّهُ وَرَسُولُهُ أَمْرًا أَنْ يَكُونَ لَهُمُ
الْخِيَرَةُ مِنْ أَمْرِهِمْ

It is not for a believing man or woman – when Allah and His Messenger decree a matter – to have any other choice in that matter.[183]

Allah ﷻ said:

يَـٰٓأَيُّهَا ٱلَّذِينَ ءَامَنُوٓا۟ أَطِيعُوا۟ ٱللَّهَ وَأَطِيعُوا۟ ٱلرَّسُولَ وَأُو۟لِى ٱلْأَمْرِ مِنكُمْ فَإِن
تَنَـٰزَعْتُمْ فِى شَىْءٍ فَرُدُّوهُ إِلَى ٱللَّهِ وَٱلرَّسُولِ إِن كُنتُمْ تُؤْمِنُونَ بِٱللَّهِ وَٱلْيَوْمِ
ٱلْـَٔاخِرِ ذَٰلِكَ خَيْرٌ وَأَحْسَنُ تَأْوِيلًا

O believers! Obey Allah and obey the Messenger and those in authority among you. Should you disagree on anything, then refer it to Allah and His Messenger, if you truly believe in Allah and the Last Day. This is the best and fairest resolution.[184]

---

[181] *Al-Shūrā*, 42:10.
[182] *Al-Nisā'*, 4:65.
[183] *Al-Aḥzāb*, 33:36.
[184] *Al-Nisā'*, 4:59.

Throughout the journey of a couple's life together, holding firm to the Guidance of Allah ﷻ and His Messenger ﷺ is of paramount importance. Bombarded with various pieces of contradicting advice, recommendations, suggestions, and societal expectations, it is essential for a couple to establish a firm foundation rooted in the divine teachings.

By aligning their hearts and minds with the teachings of Allah ﷻ, a couple embraces the principle of submitting willingly and humbly to His Decree. This approach becomes the compass that allows the couple to navigate the turbulent waters of disagreements and conflicts. Instead of engaging in an endless cycle of debate and contention, they find solace and resolution in the clarity provided by divine guidance.

By placing their trust in Allah's Wisdom, the couple embraces the notion that ultimate decision-making lies in the hands of the Creator. No longer burdened by the interminable struggle to determine who should have the final say in a matter, they are freed from the shackles of ego and personal bias. When their common criterion becomes the divinely ordained principles, unity, harmony, and a shared sense of purpose naturally bloom forth from the soil of faith.

If a marriage is built upon a bedrock of obedience to Allah ﷻ, and both husband and wife have set that as a genuine intention from the outset of the relationship, then Allah ﷻ will Himself assist this couple in their journey, even if they lack many of the ingredients of a successful marriage. If, however, this couple build their relationship upon anything less, then Shayṭān will take it upon himself to separate them sooner or later, even if their marriage had all the ingredients of a successful marriage.

Who is better placed to be the ultimate reference point in your relationship than the One who said:

وَلَا يُنَبِّئُكَ مِثْلُ خَبِيرٍ

And no one can inform you [O Prophet] like the All-Knowledgeable.[185]

On giving and receiving advice

In many relationships, a spouse may try and offer the other their advice on a matter, but the resulting facial and verbal expressions from their spouse make it clear as daylight that their advice was counterproductive, despite both the content and mannerism of that advice being on point. So, what happens? They will often stop giving advice altogether to avoid such a reaction, and as a result, the issue is never resolved. Consequently, a sense of bitterness and spite may begin to develop which, in many cases, can erupt later in a fit of rage.

Many couples are perfectly able to discuss any topic under the sun amicably. Often however, the moment the topic of religion is brought up by one spouse, the other perceives tension, anxiety and discomfort. The husband hears "religion" and recoils, thinking that his leadership is being undermined because he should know it all. Similarly, a wife may hear "religion" and suffer a similar angst as she interprets this as being unromantic or an expression of her husband's desire to control her. There are many deep-rooted reasons why bringing the topic of Islam into a conversation may elicit negative reactions of discomfort. Perhaps your spouse has undergone traumatic past experiences, perceives painful associations with the topic, or has witnessed Islam being misused by others to threaten and abuse. The roots of these reactions must be explored individually and unpacked so you can understand why your spouse finds "Islam" to be a triggering word. Self-reflection, inner purification, and healing are vital components of a strong marriage. This involves forcing

[185] *Fāṭir*, 35:14.

yourself to confront uncomfortable realities that may be blocking your personal development.

Generally speaking, sincere advice should be presented and received as a gift, and as such, ought to be carefully gift wrapped and given in a thoughtful way that does not offend others.

ʿUmar ibn al-Khaṭṭāb ﵁ once said:

رَحِمَ اللَّهُ امْرَأً أَهْدَى إِلَيْنَا مَسَاوِئَنَا

May Allah have mercy on a person who gifts me with my faults.[186]

Secondly, though a husband and wife may disagree all day long about other topics, there should be a level of humility, respect, and restraint when religion is spoken of. The rejection of sound advice is a sign of underlying arrogance and a worrying indicator of the spiritual trajectory of a believer.

ʿAbdullāh ibn Masʿūd ﵁ likewise said:

إِنَّ مِنْ أَكْبَرِ الذَّنْبِ أَنْ يَقُولَ الرَّجُلُ لِأَخِيهِ: اِتَّقِ اللهَ، فَيَقُولُ: عَلَيْكَ بِنَفْسِكَ! أَنْتَ تَأْمُرُنِي؟

Verily, one of the greatest sins is when a person says to his brother, "Fear Allah," and the brother responds, "Mind your own self, who are you to advise me?"[187]

Speaking about the hypocrites, Allah ﷻ said:

وَإِذَا قِيلَ لَهُ اتَّقِ اللَّهَ أَخَذَتْهُ الْعِزَّةُ بِالْإِثْمِ فَحَسْبُهُ جَهَنَّمُ وَلَبِئْسَ الْمِهَادُ

When it is said to them, "Fear Allah," pride carries them off to sin. Hell will be their proper place. What an evil place to rest! [188]

[186] Al-Māwardī, *Adab al-Dunyā wa al-Dīn.*
[187] Al-Ṭabarānī, *Muʿjam al-Kabīr li al-Ṭabarānī.*
[188] *Al-Baqarah* 2:206

The Prophet Muhammad ﷺ likewise issued a dire warning on the threat of arrogance:

لَا يَدْخُلُ الْجَنَّةَ مَنْ كَانَ فِي قَلْبِهِ مِثْقَالُ ذَرَّةٍ مِنْ كِبْرٍ. قَالَ رَجُلٌ: إِنَّ الرَّجُلَ يُحِبُّ أَنْ يَكُونَ ثَوْبُهُ حَسَنًا وَنَعْلُهُ حَسَنَةً، قَالَ: إِنَّ اللهَ جَمِيلٌ يُحِبُّ الْجَمَالَ، الْكِبْرُ بَطَرُ الْحَقِّ، وَغَمْطُ النَّاسِ.

"Whoever has even an atom's weight of arrogance in their heart will not enter Paradise." A man asked, "O Messenger of Allah, what about a person who loves to have nice clothes and shoes?" The Prophet replied, "Verily, Allah is Beautiful and loves beauty. Arrogance is rejecting the truth and looking down upon people."[189]

Religious blackmailing

This principle of "return it back to Allah and His Messenger if you believe in Allah and the Last Day" should never be misunderstood as a justification for religious blackmailing, which will invariably cause huge issues between the couple – particularly practicing couples – not just in their relationship with one another, but also their relationship with Islam. For example, a husband, may weaponise Islamic text on the topic of obedience to the husband, such that his wife constantly feels that she is courting the Wrath of Allah ﷻ, yet confused because she is, in her mind, unable to harmonise between this instruction to obey the husband on one hand and his many failings towards her on the other. Similarly, the wife may quote the following Hadith against her husband:

خَيْرُكُمْ خَيْرُكُمْ لِأَهْلِهِ وَأَنَا خَيْرُكُمْ لِأَهْلِي

The best of you are the best to their families, and I am the best to my family.[190]

[189] Muslim, *Ṣaḥīḥ Muslim*.

[190] Al-Tirmidhī, *Jāmiʿ al-Tirmidhī*.

Armed with this narration, she may jump on every opportunity to remind her husband of how inadequate he is every time he disappoints her, whether because he comes home late from work, visits friends, or struggles with finances. Weaponising religion to harm your spouse not only shatters your relationship, but compromises your own and their relationship with Allah ﷻ as a result of creating a false association between fear, pain, and religion. This is a harmful connection that Islam did not make, and can ultimately push your spouse away from religion.

There is hardly ever a marriage ceremony except that the shaykh conducting it will solemnise the union with the words, "Upon you is the book of Allah ﷻ and the Sunnah of the Messenger of Allah ﷺ." Despite every marital contract featuring this statement, the subsequent spousal disputes make it patently obvious that both parties need to look deeper into what the Book of Allah ﷻ and the Sunnah of His Messenger ﷺ actually have to say about an Islamic marriage.

In the wake of every dispute, the first question you both must answer is, "What does Allah want from me?" And after learning, reflecting, and discovering what the answer to that question is, endeavour to submit to it willingly and with an open heart.

Putting this principle into practice

Get familiar with the true sources of authority

Choose any abridged Qur'anic commentary (tafsīr) in your spoken language and go through, to begin with, the tafsīr of Juz' ʿAmma together. Then, read the Hadith Collection Riyāḍ al-Ṣāliḥīn, reflecting on what you are reading via mutual discussions with each other. By sincerely engaging with these texts, you are laying the foundation for the transformation of your hearts. Through these mutual discussions, reflections, and pondering, we kindle a love for both the Qur'an and Prophetic traditions. This love will instil in you, as a couple, a sense of trust and respect for these sacred sources, thus compelling you to prioritise their teachings as the ultimate guide to life.

Engage in self-reflection and self-accountability

Before seeking a resolution to any disputes with your spouse, engage in self-reflection and self-accountability, making sure to address the inner obstacles that prevent you from heeding advice or accepting an Islamic judgement that may not favour your ego. During a heated conflict, observe a moment of introspective silence in which you honestly assess your role in the dispute, acknowledge any biases you may have, assess your own sincerity, and confront the inner demons of arrogance that prevent your heart from submitting to what is right.

Undoubtedly, your initial failures in this endeavour may appear insurmountable, as self-confrontation is a challenging task. However, with perseverance and the passing of time, this practice will gradually become second nature and facilitate the steady transformation of your heart and the emergence of a new paradigm in your marriage.

CHAPTER SEVENTEEN

On remembering the goodness

وَلَا تَنسَوُا۟ ٱلْفَضْلَ بَيْنَكُمْ

And do not forget the graciousness between you.[191]

A jurist I know, reflecting upon his experience serving as a judge, astutely observed that the failure to apply this principle is the root cause of the vast majority of marital conflicts. In the heat of a dispute, the virtues and noble qualities of one's spouse are often forgotten and denied. Questions that should naturally arise in times of pain and sorrow, such as "What happened to the beautiful moments we shared?" or "What happened to the years of unwavering support for each other and the family?" are shamefully overlooked.

The context of this instruction is as follows.

Allah ﷻ said:

وَإِن طَلَّقْتُمُوهُنَّ مِن قَبْلِ أَن تَمَسُّوهُنَّ وَقَدْ فَرَضْتُمْ لَهُنَّ فَرِيضَةً فَنِصْفُ
مَا فَرَضْتُمْ إِلَّآ أَن يَعْفُونَ أَوْ يَعْفُوَا۟ ٱلَّذِى بِيَدِهِۦ عُقْدَةُ ٱلنِّكَاحِ

[191] *Al-Baqarah*, 2:237.

And if you divorce them before consummating the marriage and you had already decided on a dowry, then pay half of the dowry, unless the wife graciously waives it or the husband graciously pays in full.[192]

So, the verse speaks of a case of a woman who was married to a man and a dowry was agreed upon (regardless of whether it was given or not). However, should the husband divorce her before they consummate the marriage, half the dowry would be paid to her, unless the wife or husband choose to waive their right. Allah ﷻ reminds us that:

وَأَن تَعْفُوٓا۟ أَقْرَبُ لِلتَّقْوَىٰ

To waive your right is closer to righteousness.

So, for the wife to say, "Take back the half you paid me", or for the husband to say, "Take the other half and have the dowry in full" is closer to righteousness. See how Allah ﷻ nurtures His creation to rise to the higher levels of nobility and excellent character, even in the context of dispute and separation. Despite such a couple being at the cusp of divorce, nevertheless, Allah ﷻ encourages His servants to waive their personal rights. Completing the aforementioned discourse, Allah ﷻ says:

وَلَا تَنسَوُا۟ ٱلْفَضْلَ بَيْنَكُمْ ۚ إِنَّ ٱللَّهَ بِمَا تَعْمَلُونَ بَصِيرٌ

And do not forget kindness among yourselves. Surely Allah is All-Seeing of what you do.[193]

One of the ways of interpreting this *āyah* is:

لَا تَنْسَوْا الإِحْسَانَ الكَائِنَ بَيْنَكُمْ مِنْ قَبْلُ وَلْيَكُنْ مِنْكُمْ عَلَى ذِكْرٍ

---

[192] *Al-Baqarah*, 2:237.
[193] *Al-Baqarah*, 2:237.

> Do not forget the graciousness that existed between you in the past and be in constant remembrance of it.[194]

Think about it: what experiences do such a couple really share together? They do not have children together – in fact, they have never even shared a bed. What possible grace could exist between them such that they are being told not to forget about it? It would be nothing more than the cordial formalities and chaperoned conversations that take place before marriage. Yet, despite that, Allah ﷻ said, "Do not forget the graciousness between you" in order to encourage believers to waive their right of the dowry and give the second half of it to her (for the man), or to return the first half of it back to him (for the woman).

So what then could be said of a couple who have been married for years, who have shared countless warm experiences, intimate moments, moments of sacrifice, laughter and, most profoundly, raised children together. If a stranger saw you carrying a heavy bag of rice and said, "Give it here, let me carry it to the car for you", you'd never forget that favour till the day you die. What about your wife who carried your child for you in her womb for nine months? Similarly, for sisters, if a stranger were to unexpectedly pay for your shopping, it would leave a lasting impression on your memory. But have you ever paused to consider the immeasurable value of your husband's spending on you?

That is why Allah ﷻ said, "Do not forget the graciousness between you", meaning the graciousness of the past is always there, you just need to make sure that you do not forget it.

Furthermore, if Allah ﷻ is instructing the couple to not forget the graciousness that existed during their marriage as they undergo the process of divorce, then what instructions might be given to those who are still married?

---

[194] Al-Ālūsī, *Rūḥ al-Maʿānī.*

For this reason, the Prophet ﷺ warned both the men and women against the danger of failing to see the good in their spouses. As for the men, he ﷺ said:

لاَ يَفْرَكْ مُؤْمِنٌ مُؤْمِنَةً إِنْ كَرِهَ مِنْهَا خُلُقًا رَضِيَ مِنْهَا آخَرَ

No believing man should hate a believing woman. If he dislikes one of her characteristics, then he certainly likes others.[195]

Similarly, when the Prophet ﷺ was asked why it was that the majority of the inhabitants of the Fire were women, he responded:

يَكْفُرْنَ العَشِيرَ وَيَكْفُرْنَ الإِحْسَانَ لَوْ أَحْسَنْتَ إِلَى إِحْدَاهُنَّ الدَّهْرَ ثُمَّ رَأَتْ مِنْكَ شَيْئًا، قالَتْ: مَا رَأَيْتُ مِنْكَ خَيْرًا قَطُّ

They show ingratitude to their husbands and ingratitude towards kindness. Should you do a lifetime's worth of good to her, and then she sees in you a matter against her liking, she says, "I have never seen any good from you."[196]

This sweeping statement of ingratitude, according to the Hadith, may plunge a person into the depths of Hellfire, and both spouses can be just as guilty of this. Yes, there may be faults, but as soon as you sensibly begin to enumerate the virtues of your other half, you will realise that Allah ﷻ has in fact gifted you with an incredibly rare treasure.

An old woman once came to the Prophet ﷺ, and he greeted her with tremendous warmth. He asked her, "How are you? How have you been after us?" She responded, "We are all well, may my mother and father be sacrificed for you." When she left, 'Ā'ishah ﵂ exclaimed to the Prophet ﷺ, "O Messenger of Allah, you gave this lady so much attention!" He ﷺ responded:

---

[195] Muslim, *Ṣaḥīḥ Muslim.*

[196] Al-Bukhārī, *Ṣaḥīḥ al-Bukhārī;* Muslim, *Ṣaḥīḥ Muslim.*

إِنَّهَا كَانَتْ تَأْتِينَا زَمَنَ خَدِيجَةَ وَإِنَّ حُسْنَ العَهْدِ مِنَ الإِيمَانِ

O ʿĀʾishah, she used to visit us during the days of Khadījah, and taking care of old ties is from *īmān*.[197]

To those observing that scene, she was just an ordinary old woman but to the Prophet ﷺ, she was a woman worthy of special attention as she reminded him of the days of Khadījah ﵂ – a beautiful example of the Prophet ﷺ upholding the Qurʾanic principle "Do not forget the graciousness between you."

A brother once shared a remarkable story of how he found himself burdened with a debt of approximately £15,000, causing immense stress and worry. However, one evening, his wife surprised him by presenting him with the entire sum. Astonished, he inquired about the source of the funds. In a heartfelt response, she revealed that it was accumulated from the sporadic amounts of money he had given her throughout their married life. She had diligently saved these funds, anticipating a moment like this, and graciously offered it to him as a gift.

Can such a virtue ever be denied?

This is a monetary example, yet if you were to apply this principle of "Do not forget the graciousness between you" to the entirety of your marital life, you will discover that your spouse has in fact been offering you things that are far more precious than money.

A scholar I came across shared a remarkable story about a man who, despite divorcing his wife, chose to handle the situation in a profoundly noble manner. He arranged for his former wife and children to reside in the apartment above his own, taking full responsibility for all expenses, including rent, electricity, water,

---

[197] Al-Bayhaqī, *Al-Sunan al-Kubrā li al-Bayhaqī*.

and other bills. This selfless act went beyond the expectations of societal norms, as it showcased his unwavering commitment to respecting the years of goodness they had shared together.

Despite the challenges they faced and the impracticality of continuing to live together as a couple growing ever more arduous, he adamantly refused to let go of the beautiful memories and the bond they had cultivated during their years of marriage. He recognised that their journey together included moments of joy, unwavering loyalty, and selfless sacrifices that should not be easily forgotten or discarded. By maintaining this hidden arrangement, many members of their community remained unaware of their divorce, as their continued support and care for one another shone through the apparent end of their marriage.

I also came across a remarkable story of a brother from the Gulf who was married to a woman and was blessed with seven children. As time went on, his wife developed Parkinson's disease, and began experiencing occasional paralysis and fainting spells. In the face of these challenges, the husband took on the role of a devoted caretaker, attending to her every need. He became her support system, bathing her, dressing her, turning her from side to side while she slept, and even hand-feeding her.

In the midst of this profound trial, something truly extraordinary happened. The husband's love for his wife deepened like never before. Rather than feeling burdened or overwhelmed, he found his affection for her intensifying with each passing day. In fact, his love for her grew to such an extent that he fervently prayed to Allah ﷻ, asking that his own life be taken before hers. He could not fathom the thought of a life without her by his side. Due to the deep appreciation that he held in his heart for the graciousness that existed between them throughout their marriage, this immense adversity only served to strengthen their connection.

Putting this principle into practice

Increase your quality of life by extending this principle further

Our lives are merged with many different types of relationships, whether it be marriage, parenthood, brother/sisterhood, employment, friendship, academia, and many others. All relationships are tested with good times and difficult ones, so use this Qur'anic principle during every one of these relationships-especially when things risk going sour between you. Even if sadly, a relationship does come to an end, you can still uphold this principle simply by how you choose to remember them within yourself.

Imam al-Shāfiʿī ﵀ said:

الحُرُّ مَنْ حَفِظَ وِدَادَ لَحْظَةٍ وَمَنْ أَفَادَهُ لَفْظَةً

The virtuous one is he who never forgets a person with whom he shared a moment of love, nor a person who benefitted him with even one word.

Upholding this is a gift you will give yourself first and foremost, as you cleanse your heart of lingering negativity and resentment, replacing it with fondness and active gratitude.

CHAPTER EIGHTEEN

On preparing for unexpected outcomes

لَا تَدْرِي لَعَلَّ اللَّهَ يُحْدِثُ بَعْدَ ذَلِكَ أَمْرًا

You never know – perhaps Allah will bring about a new situation.[198]

This verse pertains to a ruling where a husband has divorced his wife in which Allah ﷻ declared:

يَـٰٓأَيُّهَا ٱلنَّبِىُّ إِذَا طَلَّقْتُمُ ٱلنِّسَآءَ فَطَلِّقُوهُنَّ لِعِدَّتِهِنَّ وَأَحْصُوا۟ ٱلْعِدَّةَ ۖ وَٱتَّقُوا۟ ٱللَّهَ رَبَّكُمْ ۖ لَا تُخْرِجُوهُنَّ مِنۢ بُيُوتِهِنَّ وَلَا يَخْرُجْنَ إِلَّآ أَن يَأْتِينَ بِفَـٰحِشَةٍ مُّبَيِّنَةٍ ۚ وَتِلْكَ حُدُودُ ٱللَّهِ ۚ وَمَن يَتَعَدَّ حُدُودَ ٱللَّهِ فَقَدْ ظَلَمَ نَفْسَهُۥ ۚ لَا تَدْرِى لَعَلَّ ٱللَّهَ يُحْدِثُ بَعْدَ ذَٰلِكَ أَمْرًا

O Prophet! [Instruct the believers] When you divorce women, then divorce them with concern for their waiting period, and count it accurately. And fear Allah, your Lord. Do not force them out of their homes, nor should they leave – unless they commit a blatant misconduct. These are the limits set by Allah. And whoever transgresses Allah's limits has truly wronged his own soul. You never know, perhaps Allah will bring about a new situation.[199]

198 *Al-Ṭalāq*, 65:1.
199 *Al-Ṭalāq*, 65:1.

So, when the waiting period following divorce – which, according to this verse, should be within the marital home (as a general rule) – has been initiated, the wisdom is then given through the words "You never know – perhaps Allah will bring about a new situation." In other words, perhaps the husband who has divorced his wife may change his mind and rebuild the marriage before the end of her waiting period. Do not close the doors for reconciliation or assume that the relationship cannot be mended, no matter how unlikely this may seem. The positivity in the tone of the Qur'an, even when speaking of a time when divorce has already been issued, is remarkable.

In fact, Sūrah al-Ṭalāq provides believers with a source of incredible optimism and positivity, giving much needed reassurances for those enduring the process of divorce, or any other testing challenge of life. Consider just a few of its uplifting verses:

لَا تَدْرِى لَعَلَّ ٱللَّهَ يُحْدِثُ بَعْدَ ذَٰلِكَ أَمْرًا

You never know – perhaps Allah will bring about a new situation.[200]

Make this your motto in life. In times of despair, when the weight of the world feels heavy upon your shoulders, let this verse be your refuge and reassurance.

وَمَن يَتَّقِ ٱللَّهَ يَجْعَل لَّهُۥ مَخْرَجًا

And whoever fears Allah – He will make a way out for him.[201]

The One who brought you into this predicament is the same Lord who can show you the way out, on the condition that you are mindful of Him.

[200] *Al-Ṭalāq*, 65:1.
[201] *Al-Ṭalāq*, 65:2.

وَيَرْزُقْهُ مِنْ حَيْثُ لَا يَحْتَسِبُ

And will provide for him from where he does not expect.[202]

The provisions that Allah ﷻ promises for those mindful of Him are not purely financial, but also take the form of inner wellbeing, ease in accomplishing matters, a cure from an illness, the mending of a broken relationship, and so many other blessings.

وَمَن يَتَوَكَّلْ عَلَى ٱللَّهِ فَهُوَ حَسْبُهُ

And whoever relies upon Allah – then He is sufficient for him.[203]

It is not incumbent upon you to solve all of your problems, but only to rely upon Him, and it is up to Allah ﷻ to carry your burdens and bring you to a better place. Trust Him, and He will do all the work. But as you do so, remember the rest of *āyah*:

إِنَّ ٱللَّهَ بَـٰلِغُ أَمْرِهِ قَدْ جَعَلَ ٱللَّهُ لِكُلِّ شَىْءٍ قَدْرًا

Indeed, Allah will accomplish His purpose. Allah has already set for everything a [decreed] extent.[204]

So, do not rush, nor despair. The darkest night is always followed by the rising of the sun.

وَمَن يَتَّقِ ٱللَّهَ يَجْعَل لَّهُ مِنْ أَمْرِهِ يُسْرًا

And whoever is mindful of Allah, He will make their matters easy for them.[205]

Allah ﷻ promises that He will expedite the causes of happiness, steadfastness, and relief.

[202] *Al-Ṭalāq*, 65:3.
[203] *Al-Ṭalāq*, 65:3.
[204] *Al-Ṭalāq*, 65:3.
[205] *Al-Ṭalāq*, 65:4.

وَمَن يَتَّقِ ٱللَّهَ يُكَفِّرْ عَنْهُ سَيِّـَٔاتِهِۦ وَيُعْظِمْ لَهُۥٓ أَجْرًا

And whoever is mindful of Allah, He will wipe away from them their sins and reward them immensely.[206]

Your trials purify you from the spiritual grime that you desperately need removed from your life, and are like your elevator to the Hereafter, lifting you to ranks that you could never have attained without them.

سَيَجْعَلُ ٱللَّهُ بَعْدَ عُسْرٍ يُسْرًا

After hardship, Allah will bring about ease.[207]

This is a promise from Allah ﷻ, and He never fails to bring about His Promise. The darker moments of life, however difficult, will not endure.

This Qur'anic principle *"You never know – perhaps Allah will bring about a new situation"*[208] – offers comfort and empathy for those whose marriages have been rocked to their foundations. It gives relief to the scattered minds and hearts of those facing the end of their marriages, reassuring them that Allah ﷻ can bring those scattered pieces together.

This is a Qur'anic principle that, when understood properly, holds back the dam of despair and allows the rivers of hope to flow, and moreover is a principle that soothes the pain of those who argue "How can we live in the same house during this waiting period, with all the pain that I have endured, and yet I must wait for my divorce to run its course from within the marital home?!"

---

206 *Al-Ṭalāq*, 65:5.
207 *Al-Ṭalāq*, 65:7.
208 *Al-Ṭalāq*, 65:1.

It is a principle which highlights that the biggest and widest door to relief is in fact the very door that you cannot see, nor could you expect.

It is a principle that says to those who exclaim "There's no turning back from this divorce!" to keep an open mind, regardless of the outcome of this waiting period, and tells you not to only think outside the box, but live outside the box – widen your horizons, for through Allah ﷻ, all things are possible.

It is a principle that reassures the divorcee whose future seems so bleak and uncertain that their current pain may end up being the cause for a much brighter future. This principle reiterates that between your current phase of pain and the future phase of relief is a small connecting phase called ṣabr (patience). Allow qadr (destiny) to run its course while always remembering "You never know – perhaps Allah will bring about a new situation."

Beware of impulsively issuing or requesting divorce

The key takeaway from this principle is to not insist that the future can only take one form. Do not rush to issue or request a divorce. Be responsible for your words, and keep an open mind.

My dear brother, Allah ﷻ has placed the reigns of divorce in your hands for a great reason. Do not abuse this responsibility bestowed upon you by Allah ﷻ. Similarly, my sister, should you fall out with your husband, do not challenge him by saying, "Go on, divorce me if you are really a man! I dare you!" This is just as thoughtless and reckless as men hastily issuing divorces in times of anger.

Why abide by the Islamic etiquettes of divorce?

One can safely say that, if the Islamic methodology of divorce on its own was to be applied by Muslims, most problems would disappear before the divorce becomes binding. Ponder over some of the Islamic mannerisms of divorce and you will see why:

1. You are only allowed to issue the words of divorce during a period of her purity (outside of menstruation), during which you have not had intercourse with her.

Allah ﷻ says:

إِذَا طَلَّقْتُمُ النِّسَاءَ فَطَلِّقُوهُنَّ لِعِدَّتِهِنَّ

When you divorce women, divorce them during their prescribed periods.[209]

This rule on its own, if applied, will deal with countless cases where divorce would have otherwise been issued. If the husband must wait until his wife menstruates following their marital relations before he issues a divorce, they will both almost inevitably have cooled down by then. Unfortunately, this rule is rarely adhered to, and thus a divorce that takes place during a period of her purity where he had intercourse with her or during her menses is referred to as ṭalāq bidʿī (an innovated divorce), and issuing such a divorce is a grave sin. As for the question of whether it counts as a divorce or not, most scholars are of the view that it does despite its sinfulness.

So, he cannot divorce her during her menses, nor can he divorce her during her time of purity if he had intercourse during it, and he instead must wait until she menstruates and then becomes pure once more. In most cases, the time to reflect and cool down means the husband would have had a chance to reasses and possibly resolve the matter.

[209] *Al-Ṭalāq*, 65:1.

2. If a divorce is issued, the waiting period for one's wife must elapse before she leaves the marital home.

Allah ﷻ says:

لَا تُخْرِجُوهُنَّ مِنْ بُيُوتِهِنَّ وَلَا يَخْرُجْنَ

And turn them not out of their homes, nor shall they themselves leave.[210]

The general rule is that the waiting period should elapse with the divorced woman present in the family home. The husband is not allowed to kick her out, nor is it permissible for her to leave of her own accord. Allah ﷻ informed us of the wisdom underpinning this, saying:

لَا تَدْرِي لَعَلَّ اللَّهَ يُحْدِثُ بَعْدَ ذَٰلِكَ أَمْرًا

You never know, perhaps Allah will bring about a new situation.

However, an issue will arise if the wife decides to spend the waiting period at her parent's home, physically separating herself from her husband. This physical separation creates a gap between them, making reconciliation more challenging. The intention behind the ʿiddah (waiting period) is to provide an opportunity for the couple to resolve their differences, yet when they are physically separated, the chances of reconciliation are hindered.

---

[210] *Al-Ṭalāq*, 65:1.

3. The waiting period is to last for three full menstrual cycles.

Allah ﷻ says:

وَالْمُطَلَّقَاتُ يَتَرَبَّصْنَ بِأَنْفُسِهِنَّ ثَلَاثَةَ قُرُوءٍ

Divorced women remain in waiting for three periods.[211]

Once a divorce is pronounced at the correct time, the couple is then required to observe a waiting period known as the ʿiddah. This period lasts for three menstrual cycles, during which they are still considered married and are required to live in proximity to one another. The purpose of this waiting period is to allow for a potential reconciliation to occur and to ensure that the divorce becomes binding after its completion. In most cases, couples reconcile and choose to reunite during this waiting period.

Interestingly, a major change to the legal framework of divorce in the UK is the newly implemented twenty week "reflection period" that follows the application for divorce. As such, many separated couples – Muslim and non-Muslim alike – will be facing this next stage of the new process.

4. The prohibition of approaching divorce in jest

The Prophet ﷺ cautioned us:

ثَلاثٌ جِدُّهُنَّ جِدٌّ وَهَزْلُهُنَّ جِدٌّ: النِّكَاحُ وَالطَّلاقُ وَالرَّجْعَةُ

"There are three matters in which seriousness in them is serious and joking in them is serious: marriage, divorce, and taking back one's wife."[212]

[211] *Al-Baqarah*, 2:228.
[212] Abū Dāwūd, *Sunan Abū Dāwūd.*

> It is important to recognise the gravity of statements of divorce, which are valid even if made in a seemingly joking manner. Scholars widely agree that explicit divorce statements, even if made in jest, are unequivocally binding. Highly regarded narrations from esteemed figures such as ʿUmar ibn al-Khaṭṭāb, ʿAlī ibn Abī Ṭālib, and Abū al-Dardāʾ ﵇ confirm that you cannot use "It was just a prank!" as an excuse.

Furthermore, in relation to indirect statements implying divorce, such as "We are done" or "I never want to see you again", the intention behind these words is crucial in determining their impact as legal proclamations of divorce. Scholars emphasise that if the intention of the husband is divorce, then it holds legal weight and cannot be taken back.

Interestingly, most inquiries received by scholars pertain to statements of divorce that have already been issued, rather than those that individuals intend to make. The rarity of seeking guidance before issuing statements of divorce is a concerning matter. One scholar shared that while he regularly receives questions about past divorces, it has been fifteen years since someone approached him with a query about the appropriate Islamic approach to a planned divorce

This highlights the need for increased awareness and understanding regarding the severity and consequences of issuing divorce statements and should cause the Muslim community to realise the importance of seeking guidance and treading carefully in matters of marital separation.

Putting this principle into practice

Broaden your perspectives when it comes to outcomes

As humans, we are guilty of narrowing the confines of our world according to what we see, perceive, or understand. We judge reality based on what – from our limited, human lens – seems possible or likely. This restricted perception is an injustice in the sight of the Divine Omnipotence that ignores the vast, unexpected, and mighty plans Allah ﷻ has in place. We do not know the future, but we trust in a Lord that does. We must open ourselves up to the possibility that there are outcomes in store for us that we never anticipated, so for now, we must remain patient and allow the Plan of Allah ﷻ to unfold before us. With regards to a marriage remaining intact or ending, then behave in the way He has advised us, trusting that "Allah may bring about a new situation."

CHAPTER NINETEEN

On parting ways with decency

وَإِنْ يَتَفَرَّقَا يُغْنِ اللَّهُ كُلًّا مِنْ سَعَتِهِ

But if they separate [by divorce], Allah will compensate both of them from His abundance.[213]

There are circumstances in which divorce becomes a genuine necessity. Despite a person's earnest efforts to uphold their values, demonstrating great patience and exhausting all possible attempts to salvage the marriage, they may come a point where both individuals genuinely need to take separate paths in life.

Numerous verses in the Qur'an shed light on the legitimacy of divorce in cases of necessity. The Prophet ﷺ was presented with the option of divorcing his wives in Sūrah al-Aḥzāb (33:28), although none of the Mothers of the Believers ﵅ asked for this. Moreover, the Prophet ﷺ divorced the daughter of al-Jawn when she sought refuge from him. The underlying idea is that divorce may serve as a valid resolution in certain circumstances. In Islam, marriage differs from its counterparts in Christianity and other communities in which life often becomes unbearable

[213] *Al-Nisā'*, 4:130.

because separation is prohibited. The Catholic church prohibits divorce, while some Protestant denominations such as the Mennonite Christian Fellowship and Evangelical Methodist Church Conference forbid divorce except in the case of adultery, and do not allow for the remarriage of divorced persons.

Sometimes, separation can be a mercy and a door to goodness for both spouses. There are times when the continuation of a marriage may have a deleterious impact on the overall well-being and spiritual stability of either the husband or the wife. Despite all efforts that may have been made to reconcile two spouses, peace may not be realistically achievable. At times, such circumstances may be entirely beyond the control of the husband or wife, who are strongly influenced by internal and external factors that necessitate the path of divorce. At other times, the pressing need to divorce could arise due to the fact that is harboured by one of the spouses towards the other, and is no longer reciprocated, causing resentment and ill-treatment to ultimately prevail.

There was a noble female Companion who sought separation from her husband and said, "O Messenger of Allah, Thābit ibn Qays is of good character and religion, but I dislike ingratitude within Islam"[214] (i.e., she does not wish to incur sin by behaving in an ungrateful way towards her husband due to her hatred of him). In another narration, she said, "I cannot bear him," whilst in a third she added, "I cannot bear him out of hatred." It is even mentioned in some versions of the Hadith that she said, "By Allah, if it were not for fear of Allah, I would spit in his face." Nevertheless, the Prophet Muhammad ﷺ strongly encouraged the husband to accept khulʿ (a type of divorce offered by the wife and accepted or rejected by the husband).

[214] Al-Bukhārī, *Ṣaḥīḥ al-Bukhārī.*

In any case, Islam, recognises that not all marriages are meant to be sustained indefinitely, and sometimes parting ways becomes the best course of action. This understanding is supported by examples of divorce from the lives of the Companions ﷺ, who are revered as the best generation.

While the termination of a marriage through divorce can be an incredibly demanding and emotionally trying experience, it is essential to remember that divorce does not signify the end of the road in life, nor is it an indication of one's lack of worth.

Allah ﷻ promises:

وَإِنْ يَتَفَرَّقَا يُغْنِ اللَّهُ كُلًّا مِنْ سَعَتِهِ

"But if they separate [by divorce], Allah will compensate both of them from His Abundance.[215]

These words carry a profound message of hope and comfort for those navigating the challenging path of divorce. Far from the extremes of encouraging divorce or undermining the importance of maintaining a healthy marital relationship, the verse offers support and reassurance to those who find themselves in the unfortunate situation of divorce, reassuring them that Allah ﷻ will facilitate new opportunities and blessings in their lives. The compensation mentioned in the verse encompasses various forms. It may manifest in the form of newfound strength, resilience, and the capacity to rebuild one's life. It may come in the form of increased self-awareness, the experience of self-discovery, and the potential to foster a deeper connection with Allah ﷻ. It can also manifest in the form of improved relationships with family, friends, and the community at large.

So, despite the pain incurred by the profound upheaval and changes following divorce, this trying ordeal imparts a divine truth: Allah's provisions are not limited to a marriage, nor will

[215] *Al-Nisā'*, 4:130.

He ever leave those who separate without their share of compensation. Both the Qur'an and the repeated experiences of those around us, that serve as living proof of how individuals most certainly can and will, through their reliance upon Allah, create a future after divorce that is defined by happiness, fulfilment, and renewed hope.

In light of this Qur'anic principle, when confronted with the challenging choice to end a marriage, it is essential for individuals to prioritise principles of integrity and fairness throughout the entire process. It is crucial not to let the disputes that led to the divorce or the uncertainty of what lies ahead overshadow this fundamentally Qur'anic principle of justice and mercy.

Commenting on the Qur'anic principle "But if they separate [by divorce], Allah will compensate both of them from His abundance", Ibn Kathīr ﵀ qualified the word "separate" with the following conditions:

مِنْ غَيْرِ مُقَابَحَةٍ وَلَا مُشَاتَمَةٍ وَلَا تَعْنِيفٍ،
بَلْ يُطَلِّقُهَا عَلَى وَجْهٍ جَمِيلٍ وَسَبِيلٍ حَسَنٍ

> [Divorce is to be issued] without insulting, cursing, or violence, but rather he should divorce her in a beautiful and kind manner.[216]

[216] Ibn Kathīr, *Tafsīr Ibn Kathīr*.

CHAPTER TWENTY

On being mindful of Allah's limits

وَمَنْ يَتَعَدَّ حُدُودَ اللَّهِ فَقَدْ ظَلَمَ نَفْسَهُ

And whoever transgresses the limits of Allah has certainly wronged himself.

The Qur'an mentions the concept of ḥudūd, or the limits set by Allah ﷻ, approximately twelve times, with ten of those references specifically relating to marital life and divorce. This observation alone holds great significance and should act as a wake-up call urging those who have engaged in transgressions to pause and reassess their choices.

To demonstrate this point, note the frequency with which the word ḥudūd appears in a specific verse within Sūrah al-Baqarah in which Allah ﷻ said:

الطَّلَاقُ مَرَّتَانِ فَإِمْسَاكٌ بِمَعْرُوفٍ أَوْ تَسْرِيحٌ بِإِحْسَانٍ وَلَا يَحِلُّ لَكُمْ أَنْ تَأْخُذُوا مِمَّا آتَيْتُمُوهُنَّ شَيْئًا إِلَّا أَنْ يَخَافَا أَلَّا يُقِيمَا حُدُودَ اللَّهِ فَإِنْ خِفْتُمْ أَلَّا يُقِيمَا حُدُودَ اللَّهِ فَلَا جُنَاحَ عَلَيْهِمَا فِيمَا افْتَدَتْ بِهِ تِلْكَ حُدُودُ اللَّهِ فَلَا تَعْتَدُوهَا وَمَنْ يَتَعَدَّ حُدُودَ اللَّهِ فَأُولَٰئِكَ هُمُ الظَّالِمُونَ

Divorce may be retracted twice, then the husband must retain his wife with honour or separate from her with grace. It is not lawful for husbands to take back anything of the dowry given to their wives unless the couple fears not being able to keep within the limits of Allah. So if you fear they will not be able to keep within the limits of Allah, there is no blame if the wife compensates the husband to obtain divorce. These are the limits set by Allah, so do not transgress them. And whoever transgresses the limits of Allah, they are the true wrongdoers.

It is therefore crucial to recognise that Allah ﷻ Himself has established clear boundaries and parameters for marriage. Therefore, approaching or surpassing these boundaries is not equivalent to crossing any ordinary limit. In fact, in the Arabic language, there exists another expression, namely ẓulm, which is typically translated as oppression. On a purely linguistic level, however, it literally refers to mujāwazah al-ḥadd, or the overstepping of limits. The idea is that going beyond these prescribed limits not only violates the established guidelines but can also result in injustice and harm to oneself and others in this life and the next.

Tragically, exceeding limits is all too common in many divorce situations. The following are some of the prevalent manifestations of ẓulm (oppression) that oftentimes occur during or after the process of divorce:

1. Not co-operating with mediators

In this challenging situation, a husband persists in his refusal to grant his wife a divorce even though she has expressed no interest in continuing the marriage, and he himself has moved on. Despite the clear signs of their irreconcilable differences, he insists that she must pursue the legal process known as faskh in an Islamic court to obtain a divorce. However, instead of facilitating an amicable resolution, he neglects to communicate with her, intentionally extending her period of distress and preventing her from remarrying.

We say to such a person that prolonging the suffering of others is ultimately a prolonging of your own suffering, as the principle states, "And whoever transgresses the limits of Allah has certainly wronged himself."

2. Speaking ill of one another post-divorce

Islam prohibits its followers from disclosing the secrets of your fellow Muslims, commanding them to preserve and conceal sensitive information. Allah ﷻ said:

إِنَّ الَّذِينَ يُحِبُّونَ أَن تَشِيعَ الْفَاحِشَةُ فِي الَّذِينَ آمَنُوا لَهُمْ عَذَابٌ أَلِيمٌ فِي الدُّنْيَا وَالْآخِرَةِ وَاللَّهُ يَعْلَمُ وَأَنتُمْ لَا تَعْلَمُونَ

Indeed, those who love to see indecency spread among the believers will suffer a painful punishment in this life and the Hereafter.[217]

The Prophet ﷺ also informed us that:

ومَن سَتَر مسلمًا سَتَرَهُ الله يوم القيامة

Whoever conceals the faults of a Muslim, Allah will conceal his faults on the Day of Resurrection.[218]

Likewise, in the example mentioned earlier, when the wife of Thābit ibn Qays ؓ sought a separation from him, she displayed remarkable fairness and wisdom in her approach. She approached the Prophet Muhammad ﷺ and expressed her sincere recognition of Thābit's virtuous character and strong religious commitment, saying: "O Messenger of Allah, Thābit ibn Qays is of good character and religion, but I dislike ingratitude within Islam."

There is a widespread story about a righteous man who intended to divorce his wife. He was asked, "What is it that troubles you

[217] *al-Nūr*, 24:19.

[218] Al-Bukhārī, *Ṣaḥīḥ al-Bukhārī;* Muslim, *Ṣaḥīḥ Muslim.*

about her?" He responded, "A wise person does not disclose the secrets of his wife." After he divorced her, he was asked, "Why did you divorce her?" He replied, "How could I speak about another man's wife?"

3. False testimony

This refers to a disturbing situation where a spouse intentionally provides false testimony in court with the intention of harming their partner. This may include making baseless accusations of the other partner committing domestic violence, supporting extremist ideologies or groups, or engaging in sexually deviant behaviour. Such individuals, influenced by misguided thoughts and the whispers of Shayṭān, are willing to betray their own religion and blaspheme it for personal gain. The consequences of such actions are severe and self-destructive. It is akin to willingly throwing oneself into the eternally blazing fires of Hell. To those who engage in such behaviour, be warned that the repercussions of such lies will catch up to you in this world before the next. There is no escaping the inevitable fulfilment of Allah's promise – "And whoever transgresses the limits of Allah has certainly wronged themselves."

In one Hadith, the Prophet ﷺ said:

أَلا أُخْبِرُكُمْ بأَكْبَرِ الكَبائِرِ؟ قَالُوا: بَلَى يَا رَسُولَ اللَّهِ، قالَ: الإشْراكُ باللَّهِ، وعُقُوقُ الوالِدَيْنِ. وكانَ مُتَّكِئًا فَجَلَسَ، فقالَ: ألَا وقَوْلُ الزُّورِ، فَما زالَ يُكَرِّرُها حتَّى قُلْنا: لَيْتَهُ سَكَتَ

"Shall I not inform you of the greatest of sins?" He repeated this statement three times. He said, "Associating partners with Allah, disobedience to parents, and bearing false witness – or false testimony." The Messenger of Allah ﷺ was reclining, then he sat up and continued repeating the words "bearing false witness" until we wished he would be silent.[219]

[219] Muslim, *Ṣaḥīḥ Muslim*.

The Prophet ﷺ also once stood to deliver a sermon, saying:

يا أيها الناس، عَدَلت شهادة الزور شِركًا بالله ثلاثًا ثم قرأ: فَاجْتَنِبُوا الرِّجْسَ مِنَ الْأَوْثَانِ وَاجْتَنِبُوا قَوْلَ الزُّورِ

"O people, false testimony has been put on a similar level to associating partners with Allah!" He repeated this statement three times, then he recited the verse [of Sūrah al-Ḥajj, 22:30], "So avoid the uncleanliness of idols and avoid false statements."[220]

4. Preventing an ex from seeing his/her children

Speaking about this problem, Sally-Anne Burris (Director of Split the Difference CIC, an organisation created to raise awareness on the unjust treatment of men and boys during divorce proceedings) said:

Ladies and gentlemen, unless your child is at great risk of harm – and I do not mean different parenting styles, I mean, beaten, starved etc. – your child's relationship with the other parent post break-up is none of your business. You do not own your child – your child has the right to know its other parent, their other grandparents, aunts, cousins etc. What you are doing is harming your child; you are stripping away their self-belief, their truth, their identity.

Be the grown up. You chose the other parent – you do not like them, tough; your job is to understand that your child's needs are not about you. What you risk one day is your child facing you and realising they can't trust you to be honest and respect their needs. There are ways to manage this; if you can't do it between the both of you, get a coach. If your partner does not do what you want, when you want it, then tough; smile at the children, take a deep breath and let your children believe their other parent loves them – that's your job.

---

[220] Ibn Ḥanbal, *Musnad Aḥmad*.

Every time the other parent does not live up to your expectations, your child is learning to be patient, kind, forgiving and, yes, sometimes they are learning how to handle disappointment. This is good, because with you reassuring them that their mum or dad really does love them – you are teaching them resilience. When they are eighteen you will never have to negotiate with the other parent again. You want a child who feels strong in their identity, so get out of the way and let them know who and how they can be loved.

In one particular case that I became aware of, a husband experienced a difficult period of seven years during which his wife deprived him of access to their children. However, circumstances eventually led to a shift in her position, and she approached her husband, expressing her inability to handle the responsibilities of caring for their children alone. She extended an offer for him to take custody of the children. However, due to the prolonged separation and lack of familiarity, the children found it incredibly difficult to form a connection with their father. Ultimately, both the parents and the children suffered the consequences of this situation.

The scales of justice, finely balanced, ensure that actions have consequences. Whoever unjustly deprives a parent of their rightful place shall face the terrifying rigour of Divine Justice, for the principle "As you sow, so shall you reap" is an eternal truth. The very act of depriving another soul of a parent's love and presence will almost always lead to a similar fate – a bitter taste of loss and longing in the years to come. The consequences of injustice are swiftly meted out to the perpetrators in this worldly life before the Hereafter.

The Prophet ﷺ said:

بَابَانِ مُعَجَّلَانِ عُقُوبَتُهُمَا فِي الدُّنْيَا الْبَغْيُ وَالْعُقُوقُ

There are two sins that result in swift punishment in this world: oppression and disobedience to parents.[221]

The dignity of divorced women

It is crucial for the Muslim community to address the prevalent misconceptions and biases surrounding divorced women, particularly those who are unfairly viewed with belittlement or doubt and are therefore subjected to second-class treatment. In many instances, their divorces stem from the abusive and tyrannical treatment they endured at the hands of their husbands who issued these divorces to begin with, essentially making them victims of circumstances beyond their control.

It is essential to acknowledge that among the righteous individuals throughout history, both past and present, there have been many exceptional divorced women. In fact, if we look to our own noble Mothers, the wives of the Prophet Muhammad ﷺ, we find that all of them except ʿĀ'ishah ﵂ were either widows or divorcees. Their esteemed status and immense contributions to the Muslim community stand as a testament to the fact that divorce does not define one's worth or piety.

In previous times, the Muslim community upheld a beautiful tradition of embracing and supporting widowed or divorced women. Instead of shunning them, the community would eagerly seek their hands in marriage. Allah ﷻ Himself commended this practice in the Qur'an, instructing the believers not to rush into marriage proposals during the waiting period but to extend their offers once it has ended. Allah ﷻ commands:

[221] Al-Bukhārī, *Ṣaḥīḥ al-Bukhārī*.

وَلَا تَعْزِمُوا عُقْدَةَ النِّكَاحِ حَتَّىٰ يَبْلُغَ الْكِتَابُ أَجَلَهُ

And do not determine to undertake a marriage contract until the decreed period reaches its end.[222]

This compassionate approach ensured that these resilient women did not have to endure prolonged periods of loneliness or lower their standards for a life partner. The finest of men would earnestly seek them out, recognising the resilience they possessed and the wise experience they may bring to a marital union.

[222] *Al-Baqarah*, 2:235.

Conclusion

The journey undertaken

Within the pages of this book, we have embarked on a profound journey, unravelling twenty timeless principles from the Qur'an which encompass the entire spectrum of marriage. Our exploration began by laying a sturdy foundation with four Qur'anic principles guiding individuals to approach marriage with intentionality, exhorting them to (1) align their purpose with the worship of the Almighty, (2) understand the weight of the sacred covenant of marriage, (3) select criteria rooted in righteousness, and (4) embrace the inherent differences between genders.

Continuing our exploration, we unpacked another six invaluable principles aimed at nurturing and sustaining a blossoming marriage. These principles illuminated the path to (5) love and mercy, (6) mutual consultation, (7) cooperation, (8) honourable treatment, and (9) the understanding of leadership within the household. We also discovered (10) the transformative power of gratitude, which enhances the beauty and depth of the marital bond.

Acknowledging the inevitability of challenges, we uncovered seven additional principles which offer solace and guidance in times of discord. These principles encouraged wisdom in marriage through (11) overlooking trivial matters, (12) seeking reconciliation with sincerity, (13) finding refuge in taqwā (God-consciousness) to navigate difficulties, (14) mastering control over one's emotions, (15) embracing forgiveness and pardon, (16) returning to Divine solutions for resolution, and (17) cherishing the fond memories and moments that once united the hearts.

Lastly, we explored three essential principles that provide guidance when the unfortunate dissolution of a marriage becomes necessary. These principles emphasised the need to (18) allow for unexpected outcomes with an open mind, (19) part ways with dignity and kindness, and (20) adhere to Allah's limits throughout the process of separation.

Why marriage is so important

Every society is comprised of interconnected groups with the smallest unit at the core – the family. A country is made up of cities, cities of neighbourhoods, neighbourhoods of streets, and streets of families. The family is the foundation upon which society is built. If there's a fracture at this fundamental level, it inevitably reverberates to the top of the societal structure, and may potentially cause societal collapse.

The Muslim Ummah faces numerous challenges, but none seem as menacing as the disintegration of the Muslim family. In fact, many of humanity's most devastating tragedies can arguably be traced back to this breakdown.

Ironically, although considerable resources are poured into lavish wedding ceremonies accompanied by meticulous planning for these grand events, little investment is made into nurturing the marriage itself. Similarly, individuals invest significant resources into building elaborate houses, only to find themselves unable to truly live in them, because they have dedicated more time and effort to the construction of the physical structure rather than nurturing the relationships that will thrive within its walls.

It is disheartening to note that many people find that their cars outlast their marriages. This tragedy arises because obtaining a driver's license necessitates studying books, taking tests, and months of preparation, while the registration of a marriage can occur in a single sitting without any prior preparations. As a result, many people find themselves well-equipped to navigate roads but ill-prepared to navigate the intricacies of a marital relationship.

There must be a similar emphasis on equipping individuals with the skills and knowledge required to cultivate successful marriages. This would involve promoting comprehensive Islamic marriage education programs that provide couples with the tools to effectively communicate, resolve conflicts, and foster love and respect within their unions, just as this book seeks to do.

Placing marriage within the "big picture"

The fairy-tale notion of "happily ever after" is a pervasive, yet ultimately tragic falsehood. It has misled generations into harbouring unrealistic expectations about marriage. In books, television shows, and movies, individuals have consumed countless idealised portrayals of loving relationships, inadvertently forming preconceived notions about married life. Crossing the threshold after the wedding, they often discover that the reality differs significantly from their fantasies, leading to disappointment and frustration. As Shakespeare eloquently stated, "Never did the course of true love run smooth." Even in modern times, this timeless observation resonates deeply, where an attorney who specialises in divorce cases noted that the primary reason, in his experiences, that couples decide to part ways is "their refusal to accept the fact that they are married to another human being."[223]

However, with the proper understanding and wise implementation of the Qur'anic guidance that has been demonstrated in this book, the journey of marriage holds the potential to bring about an earthly joy that is perhaps surpassed only by contentment of faith itself. Surprisingly, a marriage survey conducted by three Colorado psychologists and published in the Rocky Mountain News revealed an astonishing trend: many individuals who had endured traumatic childhoods characterised by abuse, alcoholism, or divorced parents, found healing and solace through their own successful marriages. The researchers were struck by the realisation that these marriages acted as powerful therapy for individuals, enabling them to overcome seemingly irretrievable losses and resolving what were once seen as irreconcilable tragedies. In other words, there has been a major shift in focus from marriage therapy to marriage as therapy. Truly, there are few experiences in life that can rival the immense fulfilment found in a blissful and harmonious marriage.

As our journey through this book draws to a close, I leave you with four essential insights to carry forward:

Remember that the quality of your marriage is a direct reflection of the quality of individuals involved. You have the power to choose the kind of person you want to be, and your marriage will naturally benefit or suffer according to the choice you make.

Remember that it is not the issues you face that endanger your marriage – it is the deliberate choices you both make when

[223] Les and Leslie Parrott, *Saving Your Marriage Before It Starts*.

handling those issues that define the course of your relationship.

Remember that drawing closer to Allah ﷻ and distancing ourselves from sinful practices is not only beneficial for our personal and spiritual welfare, but also improves us as husbands, wives, friends, family members, colleagues, and neighbours. Our relationship with Allah ﷻ is intricately intertwined with the health of our relationships.

Finally, remember that the family stands tall as the bedrock of civilisation, an unshakable pillar that shapes both the individual and society. Throughout history, strong nations have drawn their strength from the foundation of healthy marriages and stable families. This reality holds an even greater importance for Muslims, as they have been chosen by Allah ﷻ to lead humanity with a divine mandate:

كُنتُمْ خَيْرَ أُمَّةٍ أُخْرِجَتْ لِلنَّاسِ تَأْمُرُونَ بِٱلْمَعْرُوفِ وَتَنْهَوْنَ عَنِ ٱلْمُنكَرِ وَتُؤْمِنُونَ بِٱللَّهِ

You are the best community ever raised for humanity – you encourage good, forbid evil, and believe in Allah.[224]

Such a divine mandate places an enormous responsibility on our shoulders, but how can it be honoured and realised if the very building blocks of our Ummah – marriages – are misaligned or faltering altogether? The logical conclusion to be found is that the success of the entire Muslim Ummah is contingent upon the presence and preservation of thriving, dynamic, and tightly-knit Muslim families, and that by elevating the status of the Muslim family and recognising its pivotal role, we will automatically elevate the entire Muslim Ummah to realise our divine purpose.

[224] *Āl 'Imrān*, 3:110.